D1345100

Gennaro's Italian Home Cooking

Gennaro Contaldo

With photographs by David Loftus

Also by Gennaro:

Passione
Gennaro's Italian Year

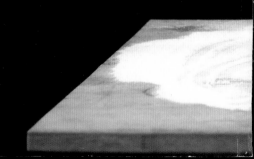

Gennaro's Italian Home Cooking

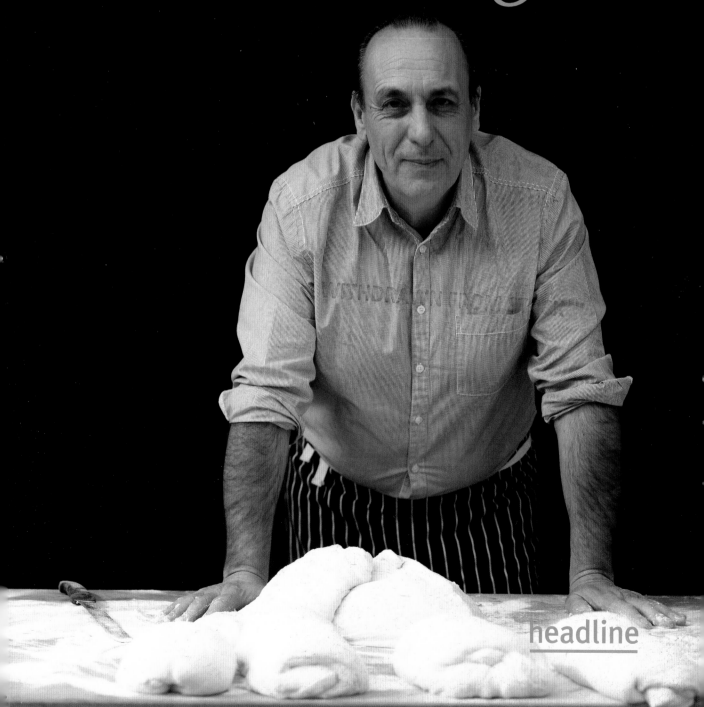

headline

To my precious:

Michael, Christopher, Dominique,
Jamie, Chloe and Olivia

First published in 2008 by
HEADLINE PUBLISHING GROUP

1

Cataloguing in Publication Data is available
from the British Library

ISBN 978 0 7553 1786 8

Design and art direction by Nicky Barneby @ Barneby Ltd
Photography by David Loftus

Printed and bound in Italy by Rotolito Lombarda S.p.A.

Headline's policy is to use papers that are natural,
renewable and recyclable products and made from wood
grown in sustainable forests. The logging and manufacturing
processes are expected to conform to the environmental
regulations of the country of origin.

HEADLINE PUBLISHING GROUP
An Hachette Livre UK Company
338 Euston Road
London NW1 3BH

www.headline.co.uk
www.hachettelivre.co.uk

Contents

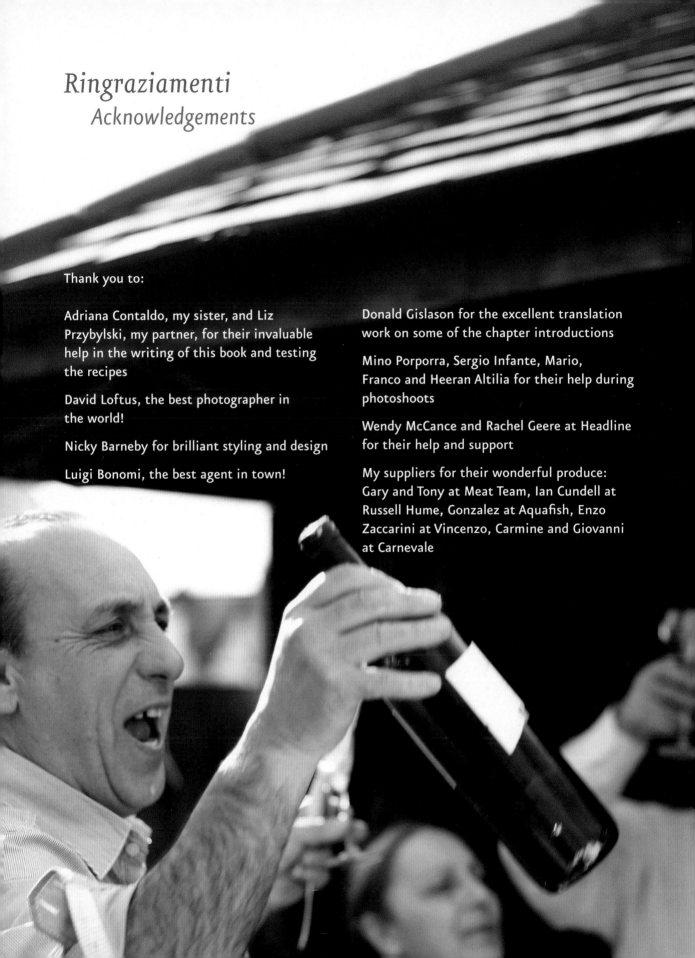

Ringraziamenti
Acknowledgements

Thank you to:

Adriana Contaldo, my sister, and Liz Przybylski, my partner, for their invaluable help in the writing of this book and testing the recipes

David Loftus, the best photographer in the world!

Nicky Barneby for brilliant styling and design

Luigi Bonomi, the best agent in town!

Donald Gislason for the excellent translation work on some of the chapter introductions

Mino Porporra, Sergio Infante, Mario, Franco and Heeran Altilia for their help during photoshoots

Wendy McCance and Rachel Geere at Headline for their help and support

My suppliers for their wonderful produce: Gary and Tony at Meat Team, Ian Cundell at Russell Hume, Gonzalez at Aquafish, Enzo Zaccarini at Vincenzo, Carmine and Giovanni at Carnevale

Introduzione
Introduction

As always, I only have to write just a few lines and memories from times long past suddenly come swimming up to greet me: the unexpected joy of discovery, of seeing family and friends again and of friendships nourished at home, especially in our kitchens.

Writing another book makes me feel young again, thinking of healthy food and happy times; food made at home, the food of Italy, the food of my region, especially from my village, the scent of the sea, the breeze of the mountains and an oh-so-happy homecoming.

I can see myself seated at the old dinner table where the family made pasta by hand, and where I did my homework as a schoolboy. This was our altar where all the members of our family sat to eat, discuss, argue, laugh – we had the best of times around that much-used table.

I remember the magical atmosphere of our house: the smell of old furniture which my mother polished continually because it was made by Zio Alfonso, my father's brother – a master carpenter – as a wedding present; the sideboard laden with bottles of homemade liqueurs and preserves – tomatoes, aubergines in oil, summer fruits preserved in alcohol, my mother's delicious jams and marmalades, olives, anchovies in salt; the smell of freshly baked bread or roasts or whatever had just been in the oven of the huge kitchen; and the sea out in front, changing colour with the weather and feeling like it was close enough to embrace you.

The sea was just thirty metres below the kitchen window. I remember that when it was rough in winter, my mother would watch it warily, not from fear, but rather because the salty sea air drove her crazy, dirtying her windows and forcing her to clean them all the time. I, on the other hand, was happy because I liked to go down to the beach and watch the foamy waves swell up and break on the rocks.

And so the sea would bring up little treasures onto the beach – or at least they were treasures to me – pieces of wood in weird shapes, strange little stones, sometimes even little gold objects. On just one of those mornings, before heading off to school, I found a gold ring in the sand, worn down by the sea, with a blue stone in it. My sister still keeps that little ring, not because of its monetary value, but as a keepsake to remind her of those carefree days of our childhood.

Spending time with family and friends, then as now, was of prime importance to us and you were never alone in the house. Every decision, every argument and discussion began and ended with cooking and eating. One of the easiest ways to bring to mind a favourite place and time is to re-create the dishes that we liked so much back then.

Over the years, I have travelled all over Italy, sampling food from different regions, not only in restaurants but also at the houses of friends and family. The raw elements of recipes, cooking fresh seasonal produce and the wonderful dishes created – to me, these are the essence of a culture.

Today you can find any ingredients at any time of the year because everything can be imported. However, I still prefer to cook and eat seasonally and get excited when the first summer peaches or apricots arrive or the fresh walnuts in autumn. It is certainly easier to create dishes now because you can read up, research and learn from all different kinds of sources. When I was young I remember we used to find out about food by watching our mothers, grandmothers, the mothers of our friends, our aunts. It was quite normal, almost required, especially for young girls, to stand around while meals were being cooked. But not only that, the smell of cooking was everywhere in the air.

The doorways of people's houses were always open so you could tell what was being cooked in the neighbourhood. And often cooked, hot food from one kitchen ended up being taken to another for relatives and friends to eat. Even today it is normal to see mothers in the street carrying pans of food to their newly married children, or to their grandchildren. It makes them happy, because passing on the flavours of their family cooking makes the separation seem less painful and the mothers rest assured that their grown-up children, despite leaving home, still eat well, which is the Italian mother's constant worry! Even when the children move abroad, they make sure that on each visit, no-one leaves without jars of tomatoes, preserves, hunks of local cheese, local sausages, salami, wine. Even though we can find almost everything here nowadays in supermarkets and delis, there is something special about bringing home food made by your family or by local producers, it somehow tastes better and makes you feel you are never too far away. And, of course, it pleases Mamma!

When I go back to Minori I love being at my sister's house; Carmelina usually invites Liz, the girls and I for lunch, and then her grandchildren come too, her daughter and son-in-law, the lady next door and before you know it, there are about 20 people around her table. Miraculously, she always has enough food for everyone and a simple lunch becomes a noisy, but jolly feast Italian-style! We often visit at Easter when Carmelina begins to prepare lunch the day before and then is up at dawn the next morning stirring sauces, chopping up herbs for the roast meat and setting the big table. Nothing is too much trouble and each delicious wholesome dish is appreciated by all around the table. The conversation is about the food and wine and no sooner have all the empty plates been taken away than my sister begins to ask what everyone would like to eat the next day! This is so typical in most Italian households and I really hope this tradition and food culture never dies away. It is what Italy is all about – good food shared with family and friends.

I hope you will enjoy recreating the recipes in this book, the quantities are for larger groups of people, which of course can be reduced, but any remaining quantities can be frozen and used up for another time.

Happy cooking and entertaining!

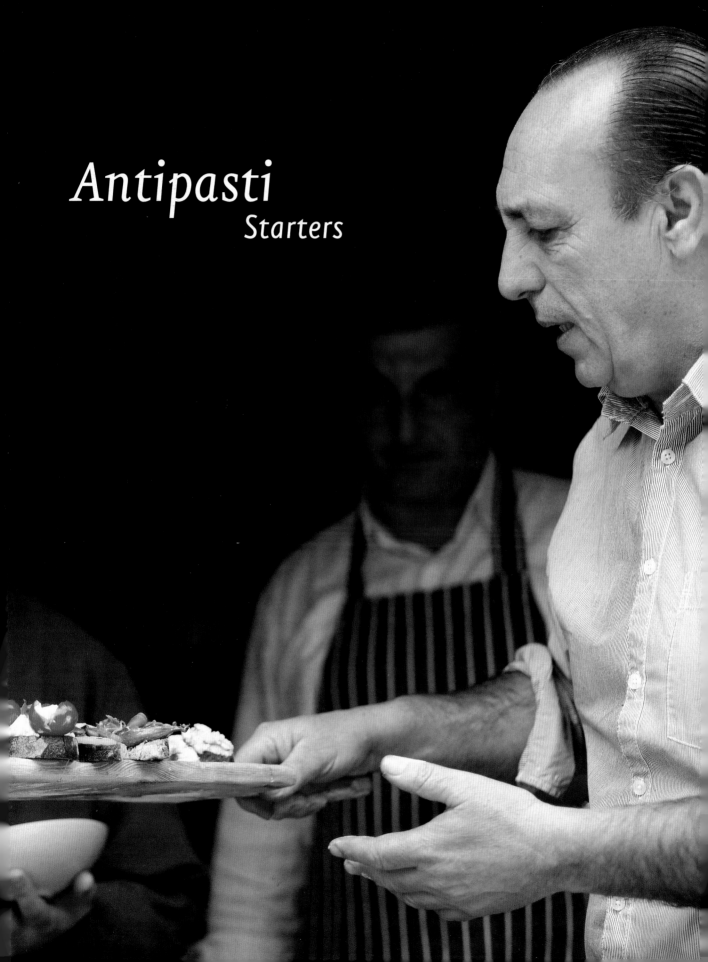

Antipasti
Starters

The idea of serving antipasto dates back to the ancient Romans, whose sumptuous banquets would typically begin with a series of light dishes – the more varied the better – functioning as a sort of visiting card to announce the arrival of the great banquet courses waiting at the door. However, it was only in the 1960s that the modern Italian practice of routinely beginning a meal with antipasti dishes became common.

Defining just what might constitute an antipasto is not easy; the important thing to remember is that an antipasto is meant to stimulate the appetite, not sate it, even though there might be quite a few of these dishes – especially at wedding banquets, Christmas, Sunday lunches and other important family occasions.

With this in mind, let's just say that when the antipasti are served, conversations start up more easily. In the middle of the table you can normally find a wide assortment of local specialities, such as olives in brine, pickled onions, stuffed olives and all manner of preserves in oil; from mushrooms and artichokes to peppers, aubergines, courgettes and sun-dried tomatoes. There might also be cold cuts such as prosciutto or cooked ham, mortadella, *bresaola* (air-dried beef), salami and spicy sausages, or plates of mozzarella drizzled with olive oil or served *alla caprese* with slices of tomato. Also popular are salads of rocket dressed with olive oil and scattered with shavings of Parmesan cheese, or salted ricotta on small slices of toasted bread. Seafood salads are common dishes, too, and might include *moscardini* (baby octopus), cuttlefish, mussels or *lupini* (baby clams); all of which are boiled and served with olive oil and lemon juice. These salads sometimes also include oysters, salted or stuffed mussels, anchovies (either plain and salted or in olive oil with garlic) and breaded sardines or little fritters made with a little fish called *bianchetto* (whitebait).

The antipasti that were served in my house when I was growing up were mostly simple, uncomplicated preserves with pure natural flavours.

Serving antipasto dishes is usually done on festive occasions. In many Italian restaurants the first thing you will be served is a complimentary serving of rustic focaccia bread flavoured with salt, rosemary and oregano and roughly cut up into large pieces. This is always delicious because it arrives on the table fresh from the oven. Nowadays an antipasto course might take the place of the *primo piatto* (first course), and in my family it can become an entire supper if it is served with green vegetables.

Preserved vegetables, meat and fish are excellent as antipasto dishes, not just for their wonderful taste, but also because they take very little time to prepare. Indeed, you can serve practically anything as an antipasto; children in particular love little pizzas and fritters because they can eat them with their fingers.

Sarde marinate

Marinated sardines

This is a traditional Southern Italian recipe that is usually made with anchovies, but as these are not easily obtainable fresh in the UK, I have suggested you use the more commonly sold sardines instead. Whether you use sardines or anchovies, this dish is really simple to prepare and can be made up to one week in advance. Serve up to three sardines per person as part of an antipasto or as a topping for crostini, and do buy them from a reliable fishmonger so as to ensure the sardines are small and very fresh.

12 PLUS SERVINGS

1 litre white wine vinegar

250ml white wine

25g salt

1kg small sardines

extra-virgin olive oil, for drizzling

a handful of fresh parsley, finely chopped (optional)

½ red chilli, very finely chopped (optional)

Combine the vinegar, wine and salt, making sure that the salt is well dissolved. Set aside.

Ask your fishmonger to clean the sardines, otherwise carry out this procedure at home over a sink and under a cold running tap. Remove the heads, pulling away the innards at the same time, and remove the spine using your fingers. Wash well and pat dry with kitchen towel.

In a large, non-metal dish, neatly lay out the sardines very flat and pour the marinade over them so that they are completely covered. Leave to marinate for 12 hours or until they float near the top.

Pick them up one by one, shaking off the excess marinade, and place them in a large container or bowl. Cover the fish with olive oil, sprinkle with the parsley and chilli (if using) and serve. If you are making these in advance, store the marinated fish in a plastic or glass container and cover with extra-virgin olive oil. They will keep in the fridge for up to one week.

Insalata di capesante e funghi misti

Scallop and wild mushroom salad

This sophisticated starter is perfect for a dinner party; the combination of delicate scallops and wild mushrooms with the added kick of balsamic vinegar is wonderful. If you prefer a more tangy taste, add more balsamic – but only a few drops at a time. Simple and easy to prepare, this dish is a real treat if you get fresh ingredients from a reliable source; in particular make sure you get good-quality balsamic, otherwise the dish can be ruined.

12 SERVINGS

12 scallops

10 tablespoons extra-virgin olive oil

2 garlic cloves, left whole

1 large ripe tomato, peeled, deseeded and cut into small cubes

180g wild mushrooms, thinly sliced

salt and pepper, to taste

100ml white wine

4 tablespoons balsamic vinegar

a handful of parsley, finely chopped

rocket leaves, to serve

Rinse and open up the scallops with a knife: cut them away from the shell and set aside.

Pour the olive oil into a large frying pan, add the garlic and stir-fry until it becomes golden. Discard the garlic. Add the tomato and mushrooms and stir-fry on a medium heat for a couple of minutes. Add the scallops and salt and pepper. Add the wine and continue to cook for 15 minutes.

Remove the mushrooms and scallops from the heat and stir in the balsamic vinegar and parsley. Arrange some rocket leaves on a large serving dish, or individual serving plates, and top with the scallops and mushrooms. Allow one scallop per person. Serve immediately.

Ficchi settembrini con caprino e bresaola

Seasonal figs stuffed with caprino and bresaola

The month of September on the Amalfi Coast is a time of change: the tourist hordes thin out considerably, the air becomes fresh and cool, and the sea becomes a flat plain of crystalline water. This is the time to make preserves, and it's also the time to harvest figs. The trees are now groaning with them and on every hill you can pick them straight off the tree without even having to reach up.

September makes figs perfumed and sugary, so they are perfect for salty-sweet dishes such as this one. The dried salt beef known in Italy as *bresaola* is not a product of the South, but I use it anyway because it is a very light meat. You can also use Parma ham or Speck (Tyrol smoked ham) instead of *bresaola*, if you prefer. The caprino cheese is a mild, soft goats' cheese (*capra* means goat in Italian) and adds a delicate flavour to the dish; if you can't get this cheese, use a soft cream cheese instead. Serve these stuffed figs as a starter with some salad leaves, or make enough for a large platter and serve them at parties.

12 SERVINGS

200g caprino cheese

a handful of fresh chives, finely chopped

12 ripe figs

12 slices *bresaola*

a few strands of chives, to garnish

In a bowl, mix together the caprino cheese and the chopped chives and beat until smooth and creamy.

Wash the figs and dry well. Slice into four sections, taking care not to cut through the stem at the bottom. Open them carefully and place a slice of *bresaola* inside. Using a teaspoon, add a little of the creamy cheese mixture too. Place the stuffed figs on a large serving dish and garnish with chives, if desired, and serve.

If you are making these in advance, store in the fridge for no longer than a couple of hours, otherwise the figs can become mushy.

Insalata di rucola, fave e mozzarella

Salad of rocket, broad beans and mozzarella

This salad makes an easy and healthy starter or light lunch. I suggest you make this with fresh broad beans when they are in season (which in the UK is from mid spring), but if you are preparing this out of season, frozen broad beans will suffice; just follow this same method. Serve with good bread or, even better, with bruschetta (toasted country bread lightly rubbed with garlic and drizzled with extra-virgin olive oil).

8–10 SERVINGS

400g broad beans (shelled weight)

250g rocket, washed and dried

16 mint leaves, washed, dried and finely chopped

1kg buffalo mozzarella, roughly chopped

12 tablespoons extra-virgin olive oil

salt and pepper, to taste

Place a large saucepan of slightly salted water on the heat and bring to the boil. Add the broad beans and cook for 2 minutes. Drain very well and set aside.

Arrange the rocket, mint and broad beans on a large serving plate. Top with the mozzarella. Drizzle with olive oil and sprinkle with salt and pepper. Serve immediately.

Crostini con tonno e ricotta

Tuna and ricotta crostini

When I am out and about and don't have much time for lunch, I usually grab a tuna sandwich. However, I am never very keen on the mayo they use, so this gave me the idea of making my own version using ricotta and a soft cheese such as robiola or caprino, and combining them with tuna to create a perfect sandwich filling. If you have time to sit down and eat, though, it is also delicious as a topping for crostini or bruschetta and can be served as a snack or even as a starter.

Combine the ricotta and soft cheese in a bowl. Add the egg yolks, the drained tuna, the lemon juice and zest and mix well. Add the parsley, basil and capers to the mixture while slowly adding the olive oil. Salt to taste and place in the fridge for 3 hours or overnight.

To make the crostini: place the bread rounds under a hot grill until golden, or in a hot oven preheated to 220°C/425°F/gas 7 for about 5 minutes or until golden. Remove and allow to cool slightly, then spread with the tuna paste. Place on a large dish, or individual plates, and serve.

8 SERVINGS

150g ricotta cheese, well drained

100g robiola or caprino cheese

2 egg yolks

250g good-quality tinned tuna, well drained

1 tablespoon fresh lemon juice

1 tablespoon grated lemon zest

½ handful of fresh parsley, finely chopped

a few leaves of fresh basil, finely chopped

1 tablespoon capers

2 tablespoons extra-virgin olive oil

salt, to taste

FOR THE CROSTINI

A few slices of good country bread, cut into 8 x 8cm rounds (or 16 smaller ones)

Crocchette di menta e zucchini

Courgette and mint fritters

My mother used to make these fritters when we had guests over for dinner. I would hang around the kitchen while she prepared them, and I usually managed to pinch the first *crocchetta* as soon as it was ready, even if it was too hot to eat. My mother pretended not to see my hand going into the pan, and then she would say, sarcastically, that the *monaciello* (a mischievous household spirit) must have been at work again. Oh, what flavours these little treats had!

Herbs used to be grown on the windowsills of every house – not least because they kept away the mosquitoes. My grandfather's house was surrounded by herbs, and in the summer when it rained the smell of the soil mixed fragrantly with the perfume of the plants. It was a fresh, clean smell that filled your nostrils. Even now, in England, I still steal the first *crocchetta* from the pan to eat, and as I do so I see my mother's smile.

8–12 SERVINGS

1kg small, hard courgettes

2 egg whites

salt and pepper, to taste

150g oo flour

2 tablespoons extra-virgin olive oil

4 sprigs of mint, finely chopped

abundant frying oil

Wash and dry the courgettes, cut off the ends and slice into thin juliennes.

Using a whisk or electric mixer, beat the egg whites with a small pinch of salt until they form stiff peaks. Set aside.

Place the flour in another bowl and mix in the olive oil and pepper, beating with a whisk until you obtain a homogeneous texture. Stir in the mint and courgettes and then carefully fold in the stiff egg whites using a metal spoon.

Heat the frying oil in a pan and cook the fritters in batches. Add a few spoonfuls of the mixture at a time, turning the fritters so that they cook on all sides. Remove with a slotted spoon, place on absorbent kitchen towel to drain and keep them warm until all the mixture has been used. When the last batch is ready, transfer all the fritters to a serving dish.

Tip: For a delicious antipasto, serve two or three fritters per person along with some marinated sardines (see page 8).

Grande antipasto

Big and hearty antipasto

12 SERVINGS

600g buffalo mozzarella cheese

6 eggs, hard-boiled and sliced in half

24 slices spicy sausage, very thinly sliced

24 slices *capocollo*, very thinly sliced

24 slices salami (of your choice)

12 slices Parma ham, very thinly sliced

24 marinated sardines (see page 8)

mixed black and green olives (of your choice)

a selection of preserved vegetables (such as peppers, aubergines, artichokes and sun-dried tomatoes)

extra-virgin olive oil, for drizzling

salt and pepper, to taste

A word here in praise of sausages and co.: until just a few years ago, salami, spicy dried sausage, *capocollo* (also known as *coppa*, it is a salami made from a cut of pork from between the head, 'capo', and the shoulder, 'collo') and smoked bacon formed part of every Italian family's larder. All of these were genuine and authentic home-made foods – given that almost every family raised pigs from which they got their fresh meat, cooking fat and various types of sausages and salamis. These pigs were fed with leftovers from the family meals (including vegetables) and hard bread softened in water. No part of a pig was wasted; even the bones were stored in salt then cooked with various types of vegetables to make a really good and hearty soup.

With a larder full of salami it was easy to just cut some up, garnish it with green olives, some mozzarella, some ricotta and 'ecco!' – you have ready-made antipasto. Today it's just as easy to do this, but for most of us it requires a trip to the deli! To make this dish I suggest you visit a good, reliable Italian deli; if you don't make your own preserved vegetables, the deli will have lots to choose from. Vacuum-packed varieties maintain their freshness quite well.

You only need a couple of slices for each person; when paired with hard-boiled eggs, bread, olives and marinated anchovies or sardines, they make a rich and colourful antipasto. I have given you my suggestions for what to include, but you can make substitutions or cut more of certain things to make it your very own antipasto Italiano!

Arrange all the ingredients on large platters except the mozzarella – which should be placed on an individual plate, drizzled with the olive oil and sprinkled with salt and pepper.

Place the platters in the centre of the table with lots of good bread and let everyone help themselves. *Buon appetito!*

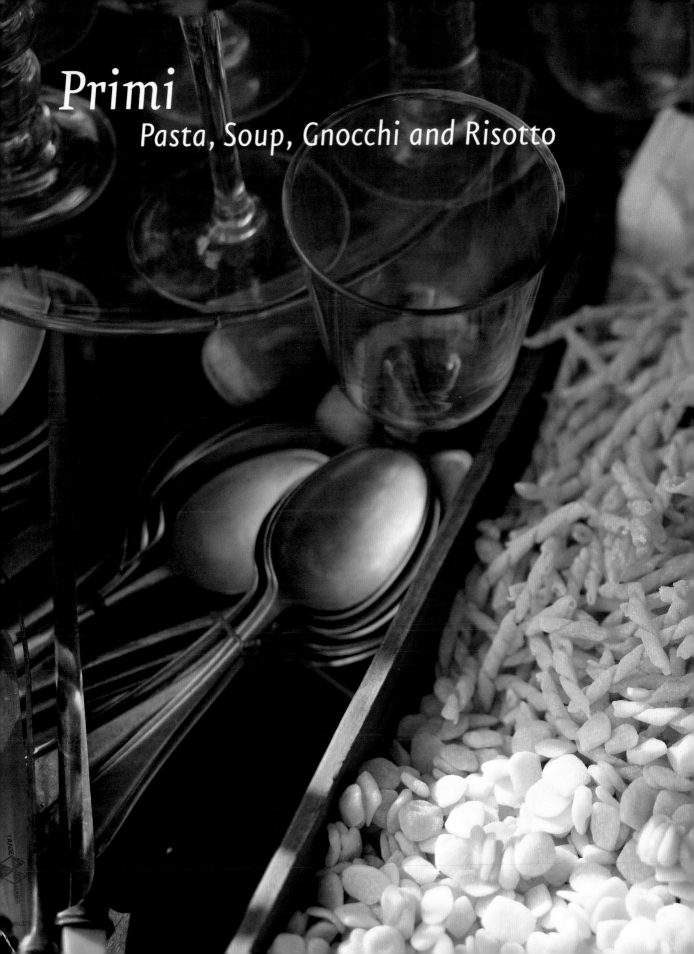

Primi
Pasta, Soup, Gnocchi and Risotto

The experts say that the people living around the coast of the Mediterranean enjoy a long and healthy life. I don't know how true that is, but my father Francesco is almost 96 and is in excellent health; my uncle Gennaro died at the age of 98, my great-grandmother Filomena at 103. So I draw comfort from the fact that I have such long-lived relatives.

The experts also say that the Mediterranean people are less inclined to obesity, to heart ailments and other diseases. They have concluded that this is largely on account of their diet, so perhaps my father is right to be so finicky about the food he eats. He keeps saying that anyone who eats food that isn't fresh, and in season, is a fool!

The *primo* (first course) in the Italian meal consists of either pasta, soup, gnocchi or risotto and is usually the most important part of the meal. For most Italians, a meal would not be complete without it.

Pasta is probably the most popular and most loved of all *primi* and its popularity has spread worldwide. Experts tells us pasta is not only healthy and nutritious, but also tell us it contains serotonin, a substance associated with feelings of peace and contentment.

My mother, of course, knew nothing of this, but when I was in a foul mood she used to make my plate of pasta a bit larger than normal. She used to tease me, saying: 'Eat it all up, and you will feel better.' I certainly didn't need coaxing! It's strange what my mother knew – without actually knowing it . . .

On the market these days, there are over 650 varieties of pasta shapes. I often think back to the days when my mother, grandmother, aunts and most of the women in the village would make their own pasta by hand, without the luxury of today's gadgets, and it amazes me how these people managed to pass on traditional recipes which are now regarded as specialities!

Years ago Minori was privileged to be nominated the village of pasta; several small factories had opened up to produce it and created many jobs for the locals. I have vague memories of pasta hanging on long canes outside to dry in the sun – every bright corner seemed to have sheets of pasta drying in it and the streets became a big yellow mass. It would then be packaged in brightly coloured blue paper. Of course, the processes have since changed and pasta-making has become a large and important industry all over Italy.

Pasta can be egg based, vegetable based or simply made with water and salt, all depending on the regional varieties. Sauces are quite regional too and vary according to taste. For example, in Southern Italy, the flavours are stronger with lots of garlic and chilli, there are sauces based on fish and of course, sauces made with our beloved tomato!

In Northern Italy, the sauces tend to be more delicate and meat based; one famous example is *Tagliatelle al Ragù* from the Emilia Romagna region. This area is also famous for its filled pasta such as cappelletti and tortellini, and baked pasta such as lasagne and cannelloni.

All Italians love soup from the simple *brodino con pastina* (a light broth with tiny pasta shapes) to the more robust with beans and vegetables. Soup for me is comfort food and there is nothing so warming as returning home on cold winter evenings to a steaming bowl of home-made soup. Even my girls, Chloe and Olivia, often ask for soup and their favourite is a vegetable broth with tiny pasta stars! You can make soup out of anything you like and it is a good way of using up leftovers. It can also be made in advance and heated up when required.

Delicious gnocchi are also a much-loved *primo* dish and traditionally made with potato. More recently, vegetables have been added such as pumpkin, beetroot and spinach. In the region of Lazio, *Gnocchi di Semolina* is a favourite dish, baked in the oven and made with semolina, eggs and lots of cheese.

Whichever gnocchi you prefer, there are numerous sauces to go with them, just like with pasta, from plain butter and sage to more robust meat and tomato.

Italians love rice and use it in endless recipes to make the renowned risotto whose popularity has spread throughout Italy, although traditionally it is a staple food from the North.

It is often made with mushrooms, saffron and chicken and can be simply cooked with butter and Parmesan or, for those special occasions, even with langoustines, prawns and truffle. I love rice and would happily eat it every day. When cooking it, it is most important not to overcook the dish; it must be al dente, just like pasta. To obtain a perfect result, rice should be cooked in just enough liquid for it to absorb and not more. I hope you will enjoy making my risotto recipes and the *Rice Salad* on page 175 for those warmer days!

Most *primo* dishes are very quick and simple to prepare and whichever sauce you like with pasta, whichever gnocchi or risotto you prefer or whichever soup is your favourite, the most important thing is you know you have a good, nutritious balanced meal for all. Without the *primo*, Italy just wouldn't be the same!

Maccaroncini con zucca e rosmarino

Macaroni with pumpkin and rosemary

This is probably one of my favourite pasta dishes! Pumpkin marries really well with rosemary and chilli. The amount of stock suggested in the ingredients is a guideline: some pumpkins do not exude as much liquid and are less flavoursome than others. In this recipe the pasta is cooked with the vegetable, so you might find you need to add some vegetable stock when cooking, or, if you find your pumpkin leaks a lot of liquid, you probably won't need so much stock.

8 SERVINGS

8 tablespoons extra-virgin olive oil

2 garlic cloves, finely sliced

1 small red chilli, finely chopped

3 sprigs of rosemary

1kg pumpkin (clean weight), cut into cubes

salt and pepper, to taste

a handful of parsley, finely chopped

1 litre vegetable stock

500g macaroni (the longer one)

Heat the olive oil in a large pan and add the garlic, chilli and rosemary. When the garlic begins to sweat, add the pumpkin cubes and stir well. Season with salt and pepper and add the parsley. Reduce the heat and simmer gently for 15 minutes or until the pumpkin is soft.

Add the stock, increase the heat and bring to the boil. Add the macaroni, lower the heat and cook until the pasta is al dente. Check from time to time to make sure there is enough liquid. If necessary, add a little boiling water. Once cooked, taste to check the seasoning and add more salt and pepper, if required. Serve immediately.

Orecchiette al limone e finocchio con bricciole di pane

Orechiette pasta with lemon, fennel and breadcrumbs

Orechiette pasta is typical of the Puglia region in Southern Italy, and it is literally translated into English as 'little ears', because of its shape. I am pleased to say I have now seen this pasta in most supermarkets in this country, so there is no need to make them by hand, as you once had to! This is a very simple pasta dish; perfect for a quick, informal supper or even a starter for a dinner party. The breadcrumbs are lightly fried, giving the dish a lovely crunchiness, and the combination of the lemon and the fennel adds a pleasant, fresh, tangy taste.

8 SERVINGS

10 tablespoons extra-virgin olive oil

2 garlic cloves, left whole and squashed

4 medium-sized fennel, washed and sliced thinly lengthways

juice of 1 lemon

salt, to taste

100g bread, made into fairly thick breadcrumbs (don't use a sliced loaf, use something firmer, such as a baguette or a country bread, or make your own)

grated zest of 1 lemon

a little red chilli, finely chopped (to give colour and heat – if you prefer a hotter taste, add more)

800g orecchiette pasta

60g pecorino cheese, freshly grated

Heat the olive oil in a pan, add the garlic cloves and allow them to become golden, then remove and discard them. Add the slices of fennel and stir-fry for 5–7 minutes or until soft and golden. Drizzle with the lemon juice, add salt to taste and mix well. Remove the fennel with a slotted spoon and set aside.

Set the same pan on a medium heat and stir-fry the breadcrumbs. Add the fennel, lemon zest and a pinch of chilli, mixing well and making sure all the flavours infuse.

Meanwhile, cook the orecchiette pasta in lightly salted boiling water until al dente. Drain and add to the sauce, mixing well. Serve immediately with the grated pecorino cheese scattered over the top.

Bigoli con olive, capperi e pomodori

Bigoli with olives, capers and tomatoes

Bigoli are long pasta shapes – similar to spaghetti but thicker so if you can't find bigoli, use spaghetti or linguine. They combine really well with this typically Southern Italian tomato sauce. I love to add chilli and make it quite spicy, but you can omit this ingredient if you prefer, as there are enough other flavours to enhance this dish. The ingredients are typical store cupboard products that an Italian household would always have available, so it's ideal for feeding those unexpected guests. It is also very simple to prepare, especially for lots of people, and it makes a nice change from a plain tomato sauce.

10–12 SERVINGS

10 tablespoons extra-virgin olive oil

3 garlic cloves, left whole and gently crushed

1 small red chilli, finely chopped (optional)

10 anchovy fillets

25 black olives, deboned and sliced in half, or left whole

2 tablespoons capers

1kg tinned plum tomatoes, finely chopped

2 teaspoons dried oregano

a handful of parsley, finely chopped

salt, to taste

800g bigoli

Heat the olive oil in a large frying pan and add the garlic, chilli and anchovy fillets. Fry until the garlic is golden brown, then discard with the chilli, if you wish. Dissolve the anchovies in the oil. Add the olives and capers and stir-fry for a minute, then add the tomatoes, oregano, parsley and salt. Lower the heat, cover with a lid and simmer gently for 20 minutes.

In the meantime, cook the bigoli until al dente. When cooked, drain (reserving some of the cooking liquid) and add the pasta to the sauce. Stir well and continue to cook for a further minute so that the pasta absorbs all the flavours. If you find it is too dry, add a couple of tablespoons of the hot pasta water.

Serve immediately.

Linguine con pesto di melanzana

Linguine with aubergine pesto

Linguine are a type of flat spaghetti and go really well with this aubergine sauce. Very simple to prepare, the cooked aubergine flesh is pounded in a mortar in the same way as a pesto. The result is very tasty indeed and a perfect quick family supper any time. The aubergine pesto can also be used to top crostini or bruschetta.

10–12 SERVINGS

1kg aubergine

10 tablespoons extra-virgin olive oil, plus extra for oiling the baking tray

170g pecorino cheese, freshly grated

30g pine kernels

a handful of fresh basil leaves, plus extra for garnish

800g linguine

salt and pepper, to taste

3 large firm tomatoes, deseeded and sliced into strips

Preheat the oven to 180°C/350°F/gas 4.

Wash the aubergine and cut it lengthways into two, making incisions in the flesh but taking care not to cut through the skin. Place the two halves on a lightly oiled baking tray, flesh-side down, and put in the oven for approximately 20 minutes or until the flesh is soft and cooked through. (This may take longer if you are using larger aubergines.) Remove them from the oven and allow to cool a little.

Scoop out the aubergine pulp with a spoon and finely chop it with a sharp knife or a mezzaluna. Place in a mortar or bowl with the pecorino cheese, pine kernels, basil and olive oil and pound the ingredients together using a pestle until well amalgamated.

In the meantime, cook the linguine in plenty of salted boiling water until al dente. Drain, then return to the pan with the aubergine pesto and mix together well. Add salt and pepper to taste, if desired. Serve immediately, topped with strips of fresh tomato and a few fresh basil leaves.

Zuppa di pesce di Zia Maria

Aunt Maria's fish soup

This was one of my family's favourite soups and the best person to cook it was our beloved Zia Maria. I always knew when this dish was being prepared, as the aroma of all the fish bubbling away in the big terracotta pot emanated throughout the village. Our cat, Mulatiello, and even our dog, Lupariello (who were both always up to mischief in the neighbourhood), would rush home and sit in the kitchen watching my aunt cooking and eagerly await some lunch.

On one of these days I remember that all the family were coming round. It was nearly lunchtime and I had hurried home because I certainly didn't want to miss this treat. My grandfather, Gennaro, was already there, my sisters were setting the table, my mother was chatting away as she busied herself in the kitchen and Zia Maria was stirring the huge pot on the stove. I noticed something strange about her, though – she was unusually quiet, which was not like her at all. Anyway, as we all took our places at the table my grandfather began to divide the soup between our bowls. I noticed him staring strangely into the pot and stirring round and round with the ladle. Then he looked up and asked what had happened to the baby octopuses.

Well, Zia Maria, who had been silent up to now, mumbled something about them breaking up in the sauce whilst cooking. As she said this her complexion turned a reddish colour and she continued that anyway she wasn't very hungry and really needed to go back to her house to finish some chores. My cunning mother did not buy that story and followed Zia Maria outside. A few moments later we heard my mother laughing. She returned and announced that the baby octopuses had not disintegrated, but that they were in Zia Maria's belly – she had meant to taste just the one, but as the soup cooked she ate another and another until there were none left! My mother called her back in, and told her to sit down and eat some more, which, surprisingly, she did!

8–10 SERVINGS

1kg clams, left in salty water for 1 hour

10 tablespoons extra-virgin olive oil

1.5kg mussels, cleaned

4 garlic cloves, whole

600g tinned plum tomatoes

1 large red chilli, finely chopped

500ml white wine

500g baby octopus, cleaned and washed

500g cuttlefish, cleaned and washed

500g squid, cleaned and washed

800g medium-sized prawns, shelled

8 fresh scampi, washed

salt, to taste

a handful of fresh parsley, finely chopped

crusty country bread, to serve

Rinse the clams and drain them well.

Heat 4 tablespoons of the olive oil in a large saucepan, add the mussels and clams and cover with a lid. Cook on a high heat so that the mussels and clams can open up. Check from time to time and remove any opened ones. Scoop out and reserve the flesh and discard the shells. Keep a few mussels and clams with their shells (as long as they have opened) and put them to one side. Throw away any that do not open. Remove the pan from the heat and drain the liquid through a very fine sieve or a muslin cloth into a bowl. Discard any bits, but keep the liquid and set aside.

Dry the saucepan, return it to the heat and add the remaining olive oil. Add the garlic cloves and stir-fry until golden brown, then remove and discard them. Add the tomatoes and chilli to the pan and bring them to the boil. Next, add the wine and cook on a medium heat for 15 minutes, mashing the tomatoes into small pieces with a wooden spoon and stirring during this time. At this stage, add the baby octopuses and cuttlefish and cook for 20 minutes with the lid half-on. Add the squid and continue to cook for about 15 minutes or until all the molluscs are tender. Next add the prawns and scampi and continue to cook on a low heat for 10 minutes or until they are done. Add the cooking liquid from the mussels and clams, then stir in the cooked mussels and clams. Add the salt and the parsley along with the mussels and clams in their shells (that you put aside earlier), and leave on the heat for 3 minutes for all the flavours to infuse together.

Remove the pot from the heat and serve immediately with some country bread.

Tip: When making this soup I urge you to use the freshest mussels, clams, prawns and scampi you can find – not only will it make the soup tastier, but (especially with mussels and clams) it is safer for your stomach! Ask your fishmonger for the freshest and best molluscs he has (it really is worth it), but if you can't get fresh, use good-quality frozen ones.

Zuppa di funghi

Wild mushroom soup

You can use any combination of wild mushrooms for this dish, such as porcini (ceps), chanterelles, wood bluewits or shitake. You can also use cultivated ones, but in order to get that 'forest' mushroom taste, add some dried porcini, which are easily obtainable in supermarkets and delis. (You will need to place the dried porcini in some lukewarm water and leave them for about 20 minutes to soften before using them.) Whether using wild or cultivated mushrooms, this dish is delicious and simple to make. I add potato to make the soup creamy and a little thicker. This is the ideal way to use up and freeze a glut of mushrooms after a successful day mushroom picking!

4 SERVINGS

500g mixed wild mushrooms (or use 500g cultivated mushrooms with 25g dried porcini regenerated in lukewarm water)

4 tablespoons olive oil

1 onion, finely chopped

1 litre vegetable stock

1 medium-sized potato, finely chopped

some crostini, to serve (optional)

Clean the mushrooms with a damp cloth and chop them into pieces. If you are using cultivated mushrooms, place the dried porcini in some lukewarm water to regenerate and set aside. Heat the olive oil in a pan and sweat the onion, then add the mushrooms and sauté for about 5 minutes. Drain the regenerated porcini and reserve their soaking liquid. Add the stock, regenerated porcini and their water (if using) and the chopped potato before bringing to the boil and simmering gently for about 20 minutes.

Remove the pan from the heat and allow to cool. Pour the contents into a blender and whiz until you get a smooth consistency. Return the soup to the pan and gently heat through. If making crostini, toast slices of country bread and cut into circles. Serve immediately.

Stracciatella

Eggy soup

This traditional soup, originally from the Lazio region, is delicate and easily digestible and so is usually prepared for an evening meal. When served as a starter and followed by *Boiled Stuffed Chicken* (see page 89) as a main course, this soup forms part of a complete and nutritious meal. If you are making this on its own (and not using the stock from the chicken recipe), use 2 litres of fresh chicken stock.

8 SERVINGS

approx. 2 litres cooled broth from the boiled chicken recipe (if less, add a little more water)

5 eggs

salt and pepper, to taste

a pinch of ground nutmeg (optional)

4 tablespoons semolina

4 tablespoons Parmesan cheese, freshly grated

a handful of fresh parsley, very finely chopped

Bring the stock to the boil in a saucepan, reserving about a cupful.

Meanwhile, beat the eggs in a bowl with a pinch of salt, some pepper, the nutmeg (if using), the semolina and the Parmesan. Add the cupful of cold stock and whisk well.

As soon as the stock begins to boil, add the cheese and semolina mixture, stirring all the time. Reduce the heat and simmer gently for a couple of minutes, continuing to stir until the egg breaks up and comes to the top. (It is important to mix or whisk the entire time otherwise the egg will not break and you will get an omelette-like consistency instead.)

Remove from the heat, stir in the parsley and serve immediately.

Minestrone di raviolini
Mixed vegetable soup with small ravioli

This is a slightly different way of making minestrone. It is quick and simple to prepare and is so nutritious and filling that it makes a meal in a bowl. It includes lots of vegetables (just like the traditional Italian minestrone soup), but I substitute meat-filled ravioli for the usual small pasta shapes or rice. Try to find the small, fresh ravioli if you can, otherwise the dried variety will suffice. Both are readily available in most supermarkets. This soup is the perfect winter warmer, and because it is cooked in just one pot it is an ideal dish for easy, informal entertaining.

8–10 SERVINGS

10 tablespoons extra-virgin olive oil

2 medium-sized onions, finely chopped

2 garlic cloves, finely chopped

100g pancetta, finely chopped (optional)

4 potatoes, peeled and cubed

4 carrots, peeled and cut into rounds

2 celery stalks, washed and sliced into rounds

2 courgettes, washed and cubed

2 leeks, finely chopped

3 cherry tomatoes

3 litres vegetable stock

200g peas

500g small, meat-filled ravioli

salt and pepper, to taste

a few basil leaves, finely chopped

freshly grated Parmesan cheese to serve (optional)

Heat the olive oil in a large saucepan, add the onions, garlic and pancetta (if using) and sweat. Add all the vegetables, except for the peas, and mix well. Add the stock, bring to the boil, then lower the heat and simmer gently for 1 hour with the lid half-on. Add the peas 15 minutes before the end of cooking time.

Five minutes before the end of cooking time, add the ravioli. Season to taste. Remove the pan from the heat and add the basil.

Serve immediately in individual bowls with some freshly grated Parmesan, if desired.

Gnocchi al tonno

Tuna gnocchi

This is a different version of potato gnocchi adding a little tinned tuna and parsley to the dough. When I first made them, I was a little unsure, but they were really delicious and even my little girl Olivia, who adores gnocchi, but not tuna, ate them obviously not realising that an extra ingredient had been added! They are delicious served with a simple, light cherry tomato sauce or you could use tinned tomatoes.

8–10 SERVINGS

FOR THE GNOCCHI

2kg floury potatoes e.g. King Edward

600g plain flour

2 eggs

50g tinned tuna in extra-virgin olive oil, well drained and finely flaked

2 tablespoons parsley, finely chopped

pinch of salt

FOR THE SAUCE

1kg cherry tomatoes

7 tablespoons extra-virgin olive oil

1 medium-sized onion, finely chopped

1 garlic clove, left whole

a few basil leaves

salt and pepper, to taste

Boil the potatoes whole, with their skins on, until tender.

While they're cooking, make the sauce. First deseed the tomatoes: place in some cold water and give each tomato a squeeze with your fingers to get rid of the seeds. Then cut them in half or quarters depending on the size of the tomato.

Heat the olive oil in a large pan, sweat the onion, add the garlic and on a medium heat fry until soft and golden. Add the chopped tomatoes, basil, salt and pepper. Mix well and cook on a medium heat for 20 minutes with the lid half-on, stirring from time to time.

Meanwhile, make the gnocchi. Drain the potatoes, allow to cool for a minute, then mash. Lightly flour a clean work surface. On it put the flour, making a well in the centre, to which you add the mashed potatoes, eggs, tuna, parsley and salt. Mix well with your hands to obtain a smooth dough-like consistency. Split the dough into pieces and roll each piece out into long sausage shapes. With a sharp knife cut into lengths of approximately 2cm. Set aside.

Place a large saucepan of slightly salted water on the heat and bring to the boil. Drop the gnocchi in and simmer until they rise back up to the top. As they come to the surface, lift them out with a slotted spoon, drain well and add to the hot tomato sauce. Stir well and serve immediately.

Gnocchi di barbabietola con salsa al burro e salvia e arancio

Beetroot gnocchi with a butter, sage and orange sauce

I used to experiment a lot with different colours of pasta and gnocchi, but to be honest I have always preferred to stick to the original. However, with this recipe the gnocchi really does look gorgeous, and you can have some fun making them in different shades from light pink to deep purple, depending on how little or much beetroot pulp you use. This dish is sometimes served at my restaurant, passione, and it is always popular. The sauce works well with the gnocchi and I usually use blood-red oranges, as they are available at the same time of year as beetroot (in winter). I have listed plain oranges in the ingredients here and I leave it up to you to use whatever you can find, but if you can get the blood-red ones, do, as they are so much sweeter and the zest has a wonderful aroma.

12 SERVINGS

FOR THE GNOCCHI
1 quantity of basic potato gnocchi, (see page 38)
800g fresh beetroot, cooked, peeled, blended and passed through a sieve to obtain a smooth pulp

FOR THE SAUCE
200g butter
12 sage leaves
juice of 6 small oranges
salt, to taste
8 tablespoons Parmesan cheese, freshly grated
zest of 4 oranges, to serve

Follow the basic potato gnocchi recipe, making the gnocchi in the normal way but adding the beetroot pulp to the mixture. Boil some water in a saucepan for cooking the gnocchi.

As soon as you drop the gnocchi into the boiling water, prepare the sauce – you need to work quickly because the gnocchi will rise to the top after only a minute or so. Melt the butter in a large frying pan together with the sage leaves. Allow the sage to infuse for about 30 seconds, then add the orange juice and some salt to taste. Scoop out the cooked gnocchi with a slotted spoon, allowing them to drain a little, then add them to the sauce, mixing well, and cook for a minute or so until the sauce begins to thicken slightly. Remove the pan from the heat, stir in the Parmesan and serve immediately, scattered with some orange zest.

Gnocchi di semolina

Semolina gnocchi

These very simple gnocchi are made with semolina, eggs and milk and then baked. This dish originated in the region around Rome, but it is popular all over Italy. It can be assembled the day before it is needed and baked just before your guests arrive. Served with a mixed salad, semolina gnocchi make a satisfying main course supper or, if you prefer, you can serve smaller portions as a starter or *primo* course.

12 SERVINGS

2 litres milk

500g semolina

salt, to taste

200g butter

4 egg yolks

200g Parmesan cheese, freshly grated

50g natural breadcrumbs

round pastry cutter, 5cm in diameter

Place the milk in a medium-sized, non-stick saucepan and bring it to the boil. Lower the heat and gradually add the semolina, stirring continuously with a wooden spoon in order to prevent lumps forming; using an electric whisk for the first few minutes will help keep it smooth. Cook on a low heat for about 10 minutes, stirring well and making sure the mixture does not stick to the bottom or the sides of the pan. Once the mixture develops a thick consistency, remove from the heat, add some salt, 80g of the butter, the egg yolks, 50g of the Parmesan and mix together well.

Place the mixture on a clean and slightly damp work surface and spread it out into a roughly rectangular shape, 1cm thick, using a wet spatula. Leave to cool, then, using a pastry cutter or a glass, cut out rounds of 5cm in diameter.

Preheat the oven to 180°C/350°F/gas 4.

In a large, rectangular, well-buttered baking dish, arrange the gnocchi in a single layer so that they are slightly overlapping. If necessary, use a second baking tray. Melt the remaining 120g of butter and pour it over the gnocchi. Finally, sprinkle all over with the remaining Parmesan and all the breadcrumbs. Place the dish in the oven and bake for 30 minutes or until golden.

Tip: For a more formal meal, use individual ovenproof dishes that you can serve at the table; they will look much nicer and will surely impress your guests!

Tip: If you have any gnocchi mixture left over you could use it as a semolina base for a pizza. Just top it with a little tomato and cheese and bake it in a hot oven until cooked.

Gnocchi di patate con il sugo di coniglio
Potato gnocchi with a rabbit and tomato sauce

Potato gnocchi go especially well with this rabbit sauce. The sauce can be made in advance then heated thoroughly before adding the gnocchi. Rabbit is quite a bland meat, so it needs to be livened up with spices or herbs – hence the addition of cloves inserted into the onions, which gives the dish a spicy taste. This is another of my one-pot meals that will give you two courses. At the end of cooking, the rabbit is removed and set aside while the sauce is mixed with the gnocchi; and the gnocchi are then usually served as a starter or *primo* and the cooked rabbit pieces make a welcome main course accompanied by a green salad or some steamed green beans.

12 SERVINGS

1 basic potato gnocchi recipe (see page 38)

3kg of rabbit, cut into chunks

2 lemons, sliced

6 cloves

2 onions, peeled and left whole

10 tablespoons extra-virgin olive oil

1 garlic clove, left whole

3 sage leaves

2 carrots, finely chopped

2 litres tomato passata

salt, to taste

½ red chilli (optional)

400g freshly grated pecorino cheese, to serve

Place the rabbit chunks and the lemon slices in a large bowl with enough cold water to cover the mix and leave for about 30 minutes. (This cleans the rabbit thoroughly and removes any impurities it may have.) Drain and pat the chunks dry with tea towels.

Insert 3 cloves into each peeled onion. Heat the olive oil in a large saucepan, add the onions, garlic, sage leaves and carrots and stir-fry until golden. Remove and discard the garlic. Add the rabbit chunks and seal on all sides. Stir in the tomato passata, some salt and chilli (if using) then lower the heat, cover with a lid and simmer gently for 2 hours.

Remove the rabbit chunks and set aside. Sieve the sauce and pour it back into the saucepan.

Meanwhile, in a saucepan of boiling water, cook the potato gnocchi until they rise to the surface. Add these to the tomato sauce, mix well together and serve with the freshly grated pecorino cheese.

Risotto contadino

Risotto with chestnuts, sausage and porcini

Although the Italian title suggests this to be a peasant dish (*contadino* means peasant), it most certainly isn't these days. In Italy, chestnuts used to be the food of the poor; in season, they would be collected to form part of their staple diet. Chestnuts are certainly no longer considered the food of the poor and make a delicious, slightly sweet addition to this rich man's risotto! A very filling and satisfying dish to be enjoyed on those cold winter evenings.

8–10 SERVINGS

400g fresh chestnuts

10 tablespoons extra-virgin olive oil

4 bay leaves

2 medium-sized onions, finely chopped

500g good-quality pork sausage, skin removed and roughly chopped

1 glass white wine

400g porcini or button mushrooms, cleaned with a damp cloth and sliced

700g arborio rice

3 litres hot vegetable stock

60g butter

80g Parmesan cheese, freshly grated

Place the chestnuts in a saucepan, cover them with water and bring to the boil. Then simmer gently for about 20 minutes until soft. Drain, let them cool a little, and remove the shell and the skin. Finely chop the chestnuts and set aside.

Heat the olive oil in a large saucepan, add the bay leaves and onions and cook until the onions turn golden. Stir in the sausage and cook on a low heat for about 5 minutes. Pour in the wine, increase the heat and allow to evaporate. Add the mushrooms, reduce the heat and cover with a lid. Continue to cook for a further 10 minutes.

Add the rice and stir well, making sure each grain is coated. At this stage begin to add the stock a little at a time, stirring well until the liquid is absorbed before adding more. Continue to do this for about 10 minutes. Add the chopped chestnuts and continue to cook for a further 7 minutes until the rice is al dente. Remove from the heat, add the butter and Parmesan, stirring very well. Remove the bay leaves. Leave to rest for a couple of minutes, then serve.

Risotto con pere e dolcelatte

Risotto with pears and dolcelatte

If you like the sweetness of pears combined in a savoury dish, then this is for you. The dolcelatte cheese, a creamier version of Gorgonzola, melts beautifully well at the end and subtly cuts the sweetness of the pears. If you don't like dolcelatte, you can use a creamy caprino (mild goats' cheese) or any other creamy cheese you prefer instead. This makes a lovely starter when you have friends round for dinner or a simple lunch served with a crunchy green salad.

8–10 SERVINGS

60g butter

2 tablespoons extra-virgin olive oil

2 medium-sized onions, finely chopped

4 sweet pears, peeled, cored and cut into cubes

700g arborio rice

1 glass white wine

2.5–3 litres vegetable stock, kept hot

300g dolcelatte cheese, broken into pieces

a handful of fresh parsley, finely chopped

freshly grated Parmesan cheese, to serve (optional)

Heat half the butter and half the olive oil in a small saucepan, add the onions and allow to soften. Add the pears and stir-fry for 5 minutes, stirring from time to time. Take off the heat, cover with a lid and set aside.

In a large saucepan, heat the remaining butter and olive oil and add the rice, stirring with a wooden spoon so that each grain is well coated. Add the wine and allow it to evaporate. Add a couple of ladlefuls of stock, stirring well until the liquid has been absorbed. Keep adding the stock in this way and continue to cook for about 25 minutes or until the rice is al dente. Five minutes before the end of cooking time, add the dolcelatte and stir well.

When the rice is cooked, stir in the pears and onions and the parsley and mix well together. Leave to rest for a couple of minutes, then serve immediately with Parmesan cheese, if desired, as this has to be served quite hot.

Risotto con pomodoro e scamorza

Risotto with tomatoes and smoked mozzarella

This is probably one of my favourite risottos as it only has a few ingredients to make a typically Northern Italian dish turn Southern – our beloved tomatoes, fresh basil and smoked mozzarella. The dish is really tasty, the sauce gives the risotto extra creaminess and I love the stringy melted cheese when you serve it. If you can't get smoked mozzarella, try normal mozzarella and if you don't like the stringiness, just use freshly grated Parmesan. The sauce is really easy to prepare and can be made in advance and the risotto is just the simple basic version.

8–10 SERVINGS

FOR THE SAUCE

8 tablespoons extra-virgin olive oil

2 garlic cloves, finely chopped

2 x 380g tinned cherry tomatoes, whole

2 handfuls of basil leaves, roughly torn

salt and pepper, to taste

FOR THE RISOTTO

8 tablespoons extra-virgin olive oil

2 garlic cloves, finely chopped

720g arborio rice

100ml white wine

3 litres hot vegetable stock

250g smoked mozzarella, cut into small cubes

First make the sauce. Heat the olive oil in a pan, add the garlic and soften. Mix in the tomatoes and basil and season lightly with salt and pepper. Cook on a high heat for 3 minutes. Remove and set aside.

To make the risotto, heat the olive oil in a saucepan, add the garlic and soften, then add the rice, stirring all the time and coating each grain with the oil. Add the wine and allow to evaporate. Gradually stir in a couple of ladlefuls of stock, stirring well, until it becomes absorbed. Continue to do this until the risotto is cooked al dente, which takes about 20 minutes.

Heat through the tomato sauce. About 2 minutes before the end of the risotto's cooking time, add the tomato sauce, gently mixing in well. Remove from the heat and stir in the mozzarella. Leave to rest for 1 minute, then serve immediately.

Risotto con radicchio rosso e taleggio

Radicchio and taleggio risotto

This is a very tasty and colourful risotto – children in particular seem to love the red, purple and pink shades! The bitter taste of radicchio goes really well with the slightly pungent taste of the Northern Italian cheese, taleggio, which gives the risotto a rich and creamy texture. This dish makes a nice starter for a dinner party or an informal, midweek, family supper.

10–12 SERVINGS

10 tablespoons extra-virgin olive oil

2 medium-sized onions, finely chopped

700g arborio rice

1 glass red wine

3 litres hot vegetable stock

300g taleggio cheese, roughly chopped

500g radicchio, finely chopped

60g butter

70g Parmesan cheese, freshly grated

salt and pepper, to taste

Heat the olive oil in a large saucepan, add the onions and allow to sweat. Add the rice and stir with a wooden spoon to coat each grain with the oil. Add the wine and allow it to evaporate. Add a couple of ladlefuls of the hot stock and cook on a medium heat, stirring all the time, until all the liquid has been absorbed. Repeat with more stock. Continue to do this until the rice is cooked – which usually takes about 20–25 minutes. Halfway through cooking, stir in the taleggio and radicchio.

Taste the rice to see if it is done: it should be soft on the outside but al dente inside.

Remove the pan from the heat, add the butter and Parmesan and beat well with a wooden spoon to obtain a creamy consistency. Taste and adjust the seasoning. Leave to rest for 1 minute, then serve.

Legumi
Pulses and Grains

Pulses and grains have been around since ancient times, and I am pleased to say that now they are experiencing a well-deserved return to British kitchens. From media reports to the well-stocked shelves in supermarkets, it is official that these nutritious foods are definitely back in fashion, in a big way!

Pulses have always been a part of the Mediterranean diet, due to their high protein content and fat-free status. Not only are they extremely healthy, but they are also very simple to prepare and versatile and can even be complete one-pot meals. They can be used in soups and salads, they can be mashed or stewed, eaten with pasta or meat or flavoured with herbs such as sage or rosemary, or with garlic, onion, salt and olive oil.

However they are used, pulses and grains make robust and nutritious dishes that give off a wonderful countryside aroma that wafts throughout the house. For me, they remind me of my home in Italy and the many traditions linked to each type of pulse. Grains and pulses are economical to use, and during times of famine or scarcity of food it was these products of nature that helped Italians to stave off hunger – which is why they have always been associated with the poor and known as the 'meat of the poor'. Quite frankly, I much prefer a steaming bowl of lentils or beans to a plate of the best-quality T-bone steak!

During the winter season when I was growing up, we often had a variety of dried pulses in our store cupboard that were purchased from huge sacks at the local green-grocer (fresh varieties were not available during this time). I loved to visit the shop and choose which different bean or colour of lentil we were going to buy – borlotti, cannellini, chickpeas, broad beans, green, red or brown lentils, and many other varieties that I did not recognise. Pulses were a regular feature at dinner during the winter. In the evening, my mother or elder sisters would place the chosen beans or lentils in a large terracotta pot and cover them with water to soak overnight. In the morning, the first person who woke up would drain the water and cook the pulses in the same terracotta pot (terracotta enhances the flavour of the dish while keeping it warmer for longer); the pulses were placed on a very low heat and occasionally stirred with a wooden spoon. In this way, my mother or sisters could get on with other chores in the sound knowledge that dinner was being cooked. Even today, when I return to my home village during the winter season, it is not uncommon to meet housewives on their daily business saying they have to hurry home as they have left whatever dried pulse or grain simmering on the stove. This is village life, where you are never too far from home – in fact, you can probably smell your own cooking pot from any shop you are in!

On the days that I was off school and there was a pot of lentils or beans gently bubbling away, my mother would prepare a slice of fresh bread rubbed with a little garlic and topped with some sauce from the pot, a pinch of salt and extra-virgin olive oil. Believe me, the taste was heavenly! I still do this today when I have fresh bread.

Many traditional recipes using pulses and grains have returned to our cookbooks now, such as one with cannellini beans or even the precious zolfino beans placed in a glass bottle (like a traditional Chianti bottle) which is known in Italian as 'fiasco'. In the dish *Fagioli al fiasco*, these beans are cooked on a very low heat with extra-virgin olive oil, salt, pepper and garlic.

Combining pulses and grains can make excellent, nutritious dishes. I remember when I was a youth in Italy and my friends and I would get together for days out in the country, our favourite dish to keep us warm on chilly days was a soup of beans and buckwheat. We would leave a huge pot bubbling away on the camping stove whilst we ran around the hills and tried to collect as many edible delicacies as Nature was kind enough to give us. We would take turns to check the fire on which our lunch was cooking. It was a feast for the eyes and palate – I can still taste the creamy texture of those pulses.

Nothing has changed today; when I return to my home village, my friends and I still organise a day out in the same way and with the same tastes and familiar faces – as if we hadn't grown up at all!

All the staple pulses and grains are now recognised as healthy and are even served in top-quality restaurants. Buckwheat, like many of these foods, is now available in the UK and I have seen it in Italian delis, health food shops, some of the larger supermarkets and, of course, online! The outside skin is usually removed and there is no need to soak it.

For me, another excellent pulse is the broad bean, which in Italy is grown everywhere. When in season (in spring), it is eaten raw at the end of a meal together with some pecorino cheese; but it is also cooked fresh in soups or with pasta, and when it is not in season, I use dried broad beans. During the Second World War my mother and elder sisters would make soup out of broad bean shells, and apparently it was delicious! I won't give you the recipe for this, but those were times when you didn't throw anything away and people had to learn all about food in order to make meals for their family.

Barley is another, most important grain, from which you can make drinks, desserts and excellent soups. In the last few years I have seen barley being used more and more,

especially as a substitute for rice. So, instead of risotto it is *orzotto*! This grain has advantages over rice in that it does not overcook and it can be prepared in advance.

There are many varieties of beans used in cooking, the most popular in Italy being borlotti – the large, beige-coloured ones with pink stripes. Then comes the cannellini bean, or *toscanelli*, which are of medium size and ivory in colour. On New Year's Eve, stewed lentils are a must, as tradition says the more you consume the more money you will make in the year ahead. For me, the best lentils are the ones from Castelluccio, in Umbria.

Chickpeas are the only pulse I know of that you don't consume fresh; they are always dried and need to be soaked for a long time – usually between 6 and 24 hours. My mother would add a pinch of bicarbonate of soda in order to make the skin softer and make the cooking time shorter.

The younger the pulses and grains, the less time they need to soak and cook. Generally speaking, lentils don't need soaking, but always check the instructions on the packet or in your recipe. Do not add salt to your pulses or grains until they are cooked, as salt tends to harden the skin, hence lengthening their cooking time.

We used to buy our pulses and grains from large sacks, but now you can simply go to your local supermarket and you will be spoilt for choice by the various different types, all nicely packaged. Some originate from European countries, others from further afield, but whichever you pick, I am sure you won't be disappointed.

I hope you will enjoy the recipes I have put together for you in this chapter – just a taster of some of my favourite pulses and grains!

Insalata di lenticchie, trevisana e carotine

Salad of lentils, radicchio and organic baby carrots

If you like lentils but want to enjoy them in a lighter way, this salad is ideal. The combination of lentils with the slightly bitter radicchio, flavoursome organic baby carrots and preserved baby onions is truly delicious! There are some really good baby onions in olive oil available in supermarkets or delis. Don't, however, get the cocktail onions in vinegar, as this would spoil the taste of the dish.

8 SERVINGS

300g small brown lentils

300g organic baby carrots

2 radicchio, cleaned and finely chopped

250g baby onions, preserved in olive oil

salt and pepper, to taste

8 tablespoons extra-virgin olive oil

8 tablespoons white wine vinegar

2 garlic cloves, slightly squashed but left whole

First, cook the lentils according to the instructions on the packet. (They usually take about 30 minutes to cook.)

Steam the carrots until tender and leave to cool.

Drain the cooked lentils and allow to cool, then place them in a large salad bowl together with the carrots, radicchio and preserved baby onions. Add salt and pepper to taste, then drizzle with the olive oil.

In a small pan, gently heat the vinegar and add the garlic. Bring to the boil and allow to evaporate, leaving approximately one-third of the original amount. Discard the garlic. Pour the warm vinegar over the salad and serve immediately.

Orzotto con cavolo nero e macinato di maiale

Pearl barley with cavolo nero and pork mince

Pearl barley is a great substitute for rice; in fact, when I first made this dish it looked like risotto and the same method is used to cook it. I have used cavolo nero in this recipe, but if you can't get it, substitute Savoy cabbage for it. This quick and easy dish is a complete meal in itself and makes a nutritious and filling winter warmer for all the family.

8 SERVINGS

6 tablespoons extra-virgin olive oil

2 onions, finely chopped

300g minced pork

400g pearl barley

200g cavolo nero, roughly chopped

salt and pepper, to taste

½ glass white wine

2 litres vegetable stock

a handful of fresh parsley, finely chopped

Heat 2 tablespoons of the olive oil in a large saucepan, add the onions and minced pork and stir-fry until the onions are soft and the pork sealed. Stir in the pearl barley and cavolo nero and cook for a couple of minutes. Season with salt. Add the wine and allow it to evaporate, then gradually add the stock, as you would when making a risotto (see page 48). It will take approximately 30 minutes until the pearl barley is cooked.

Remove the pan from the heat, mix in the remaining olive oil, the parsley and some black pepper. Serve immediately.

Fagioli borlotti e pappardelle

Borlotti bean and pappardelle pasta

This is my sister Adriana's version of the traditional pasta and fagioli dish (pasta and beans), which is popular throughout Italy in its different variations. I normally make this dish with fresh tomatoes, but I must say that when cooked separately the tomato sauce enriches the pasta and beans. I like to make this soup in season when fresh borlotti beans are available (usually late spring/early summer), which give it a nice creamy consistency. However, this can also be made with dried borlotti beans. These require soaking overnight before use, but after that you can follow the recipe as below.

8–10 SERVINGS

1kg fresh borlotti beans (that's shelled weight, so buy approx. 1.6kg of fresh beans in their shells)

3 carrots, cubed

5 stalks of celery (including some leaves), finely sliced

4 garlic cloves, left whole

2 handfuls of fresh basil leaves

salt, to taste

5 tablespoons extra-virgin olive oil

½ red chilli, finely chopped

2 x 400g tins of plum tomatoes

500g pappardelle or tagliatelle pasta, broken up

freshly grated Parmesan cheese, to serve (optional)

Shell the beans, wash them and place them in a large saucepan with 3 litres of cold water. Add the carrots, celery, 2 of the garlic cloves, a handful of basil leaves and some salt. Cover with a lid and bring to the boil. Reduce the heat and simmer for one and a half hours or until tender.

Meanwhile, in another, smaller pan, heat the olive oil, add the remaining garlic cloves and the chilli and stir-fry until the garlic turns golden, but is not burnt. Add the tomatoes, the remaining handful of basil leaves and some salt. Cook on a fairly high heat for about 15 minutes or until the sauce thickens, stirring from time to time. Set aside.

When the beans are cooked, leave the pan on the heat and add the pasta to it. (The pasta should soak up most of the liquid so you shouldn't need to drain it but please do if you feel you need to.) Cook, stirring from time to time. About five minutes before the pasta is al dente, stir in the tomato sauce. Remove from the heat and allow to stand for 5 minutes.

Serve with freshly grated Parmesan, if desired.

Cannellini e polenta al forno

Cannellini bean and polenta bake

Cannellini beans are the white Italian beans that are readily available dried from delis and supermarkets. In this recipe the beans are combined with a tomato sauce and polenta to make a healthy, but robust, dish that will satisfy your appetite on cold winter evenings. This bean bake is best cooked in a clay dish as this not only gives the food a better flavour and retains more heat, but it also lends it a genuinely rustic feel when it is served.

12–15 SERVINGS

400g dried cannellini beans

10 tablespoons extra-virgin olive oil

2 small red onions, finely chopped

4 celery stalks, finely chopped

2 large leeks, chopped into rounds

200g runner beans, sliced

salt, to taste

150g pancetta, cubed

200g button mushrooms, sliced

200g cherry tomatoes, sliced in half

200g polenta

extra-virgin olive oil, for drizzling

handful of fresh parsley, finely chopped

150g fontina cheese, cubed

a little extra-virgin olive oil for greasing

Place the beans in lots of fresh water and leave them to soak overnight. The next day, drain and cook them in plenty of slightly salted water for 30–40 minutes or until tender but not mushy.

Towards the end of their cooking time, heat the olive oil in a large saucepan and add the onions, celery and leek and fry until soft. Add the runner beans, season with salt and stir-fry for 2 minutes. Add the pancetta and cook for a further minute. Throw in the mushrooms and stir-fry for a couple of minutes. Carefully stir in the cherry tomatoes and cannellini beans, making sure not to break the cooked beans. Remove from the heat and set aside.

In the meantime, preheat the oven to 200°C/400°F/gas 6.

Make the polenta to a runny consistency, according to the instructions on the packet. If you need extra water, make sure you have some boiling water ready to add. As you are making the polenta, keep stirring it with a wooden spoon to prevent lumps.

In a large bowl, mix together a little polenta at a time with some of the bean mixture, again taking care not to break the beans, until all the polenta and most of the beans are well amalgamated. Keep aside some of the beans and vegetables. Stir in the fontina cheese and season with salt to taste.

Grease the bottom of a terracotta or ovenproof dish with a little olive oil. Pour the mixture into it, and add the remaining beans and vegetables. Cook in the preheated oven for about 20 minutes until golden on top. Remove and serve.

Tip: If you are using new clay pots for the first time, immerse them in water for 24 hours before using, as this will prevent them breaking in the hot oven.

Ceci all'acciugata

Chickpeas in an anchovy sauce

This is a very simple dish to prepare and can be served warm or cold – it makes a delicious starter or is great served at parties. The anchovy sauce really livens up the chickpeas, but please make sure that you use good-quality extra-virgin olive oil and good-quality chickpeas with a long sell-by date. The younger the chickpeas, the quicker they cook.

10–12 SERVINGS

400g chickpeas

salt, to taste

8 tablespoons extra-virgin olive oil, plus extra for drizzling

2 garlic cloves

8 anchovy fillets

a handful of parsley, finely chopped

Soak the chickpeas overnight. Drain and cook them in slightly salted water for approximately 2 hours or until tender. (Check them from time to time, as the chickpeas may take less or a bit more time to cook.)

Drain and place in a large serving bowl. Heat the olive oil in a small pan and add the garlic. Add the anchovy fillets and dissolve them in the oil. Remove from the heat and pour over the chickpeas, sprinkling with the chopped parsley and drizzling with a little more olive oil.

Tip: If you have any leftovers, mix them in with some cooked pasta.

Crochette di orzo, carote e spinaci con salsina fresca di pomodoro

Pearl barley, carrot and spinach fritters with a fresh tomato sauce

11 SERVINGS

(Makes approx. 22 fritters: 2 per person for a main course)

400g pearl barley

1 onion, finely chopped

200g spinach, washed

a handful of parsley

a few sprigs of marjoram

6 medium-sized carrots, grated

salt and pepper, to taste

6 tablespoons extra-virgin olive oil

FOR THE TOMATO SAUCE

8 tablespoons extra-virgin olive oil

1 garlic clove, finely chopped

½ onion, finely chopped

a few rosemary needles, finely chopped

8 basil leaves

1kg fresh, very ripe plum tomatoes, roughly chopped

salt and freshly ground black pepper

1 round pastry cutter, 9cm in diameter

These make great vegetarian burgers and are a good way of getting children to eat spinach. The inclusion of pearl barley means they are filling and highly nutritious, the spinach is a good source of iron and the carrots provide lots of vitamins A and C. They are delicious served with a fresh tomato sauce and really need nothing else, as the fritters are a meal in themselves.

Place the pearl barley in a large saucepan, cover with slightly salted water and bring to the boil, then reduce the heat and gently simmer for about 40 minutes or until tender. Alternatively, follow the instructions on the packet.

Drain and place half the pearl barley in a mouli together with the chopped onion, spinach and herbs. Whiz until you obtain a smooth consistency. Place in a bowl with the grated carrots, the remainder of the pearl barley, salt and pepper, the olive oil and mix well together with a wooden spoon.

Preheat the oven to 180°C/350°F/gas 4. Line a baking tray with some greaseproof paper and place the pastry cutter on it. Fill the pastry cutter 2cm high with the mixture, pressing down well with your fingers. Remove the pastry cutter and continue making the fritters at even intervals over the tray until the mixture is used up. Place the tray in the oven for 25 minutes, or more if you like them a little crispy on the outside.

Meanwhile, make the tomato sauce. In a pan, heat the olive oil and add the garlic, onion, rosemary and basil and sweat until the onion and garlic are golden. Add the tomatoes, lower the heat and simmer for about 15 minutes, stirring from time to time until all the tomatoes go nice and mushy. Remove from the heat, add salt and pepper to taste and serve with the pearl barley cakes.

Zuppa di fave al finocchio
Broad bean and fennel soup

This is a very quick, simple and nutritious soup, and fennel has many healing properties as well as aiding digestion. This dish is perfect to make in spring when the first tender broad beans are out, but you can substitute frozen ones if you are making this out of season or can't find them fresh. You can serve this soup the Italian way with some grated Parmesan or pecorino cheese and lots of good bread.

8–10 SERVINGS

2kg fresh broad beans, in their shells (if not in season, use 1.7kg frozen beans)

4 tablespoons extra-virgin olive oil

2 sweet red onions, finely chopped

4 sun-dried tomatoes, finely chopped

4 small fresh fennel, washed and cut into medium-sized pieces (keep most of the hairy bits, as they have the most flavour!), plus extra to garnish, finely chopped

2 bunches Swiss chard or large-leaf spinach, cleaned and cut into strips

2 litres vegetable stock

4 medium-sized potatoes, peeled and cubed

salt and pepper, to taste

extra-virgin olive oil, for drizzling

If you are using fresh broad beans, shell them and remove their skin, if you prefer.

Heat the olive oil in a small pan, add the onions and sweat. Stir in the tomatoes and set aside.

In a large saucepan, place the fennel, Swiss chard or spinach and stock and bring to the boil. Then add the onion and tomato mixture and the broad beans. Add the potatoes halfway through cooking. Mix well and cook on a medium heat for approximately 30 minutes or until the vegetables are soft but not mushy. Add salt to taste, if necessary, and serve with some freshly ground black pepper, a drizzle of extra-virgin olive oil and garnish with bits of fresh, hairy fennel.

Crema di lenticchie e gnocchetti di grano saraceno
Creamy lentil soup with buckwheat dumplings

Simple to prepare and very nutritious, this soup is a meal in itself. Both lentils and buckwheat are highly nutritious and very good for all the family. Lentils have a high iron content and provide a good source of protein too – ideal for vegetarians. If you are in a hurry, you may substitute pasta or potato gnocchi for the buckwheat dumplings, or simply enjoy the creamy lentil soup as it is with some good bread. Buckwheat flour is obtainable from health food shops and online.

12 SERVINGS

FOR THE SOUP

400g lentils

2 potatoes, cubed

a couple of sprigs of fresh thyme

3 celery stalks, finely chopped

4 litres vegetable stock

10 tablespoons extra-virgin olive oil

2 garlic cloves, left whole

FOR THE DUMPLINGS

150g buckwheat flour

1 teaspoon mixed dried herbs

2 eggs, lightly whisked

100g pancetta, very finely chopped (optional)

300g floury potatoes, mashed

salt and pepper, to taste

In a large saucepan, place the lentils, cubed potatoes, thyme, celery and stock and bring to the boil. Reduce the heat and simmer gently for about 30 minutes or until the lentils are well cooked.

Meanwhile, prepare the dumplings. In a large bowl, place the buckwheat flour, dried herbs, eggs, pancetta, mashed potato, salt and pepper. Mix together well with your hands until you obtain a smooth, soft consistency, but not sticky. If necessary, add some more flour or water.

Place the mixture on a clean, floured work surface, roll it into a long sausage shape and slice into small dumplings. Set aside.

When the lentils are cooked, remove from the heat and discard the thyme sprigs. Pour the soup into a blender and whiz until you obtain a creamy consistency.

Bring a saucepan of water to the boil and drop in the dumplings. Reduce the heat to medium and cook for about 10 minutes or until the dumplings rise to the top and are soft. Drain and add to the soup.

Heat the olive oil in a small frying pan, add the garlic and stir-fry on a high heat until the garlic turns golden. Remove from the heat, discard the garlic and pour the hot, garlicky oil over the soup. Serve immediately.

La zuppa di farro al prosciutto
Soup of spelt with gammon

Farro, or spelt, is a grain that was much used in Roman times to make bread and pasta. This grain is now cultivated in regions in central Italy and has become a very popular alternative to rice and pasta because of its excellent nutritional value. If you can't find it in your supermarket, health food shops stock it.

This soup is perfect for feeding lots of people, and can be served in two ways. Firstly, prepare it as a main course with the pieces of gammon in it (as below) – filling enough so there is no need for another course, just some good bread. Alternatively, make two courses from this by having the soup simply with the spelt as a first course, followed by slices of gammon served with either boiled root vegetables or a salad as the second course.

10–12 SERVINGS

1kg gammon

2 medium-sized onions, roughly chopped into quarters

2 medium-sized carrots, left whole

2 celery stalks, left whole

700g tinned plum tomatoes

salt and pepper, to taste

400g spelt

100g freshly grated pecorino cheese, to serve

Place the gammon in cold water for about 4 hours or overnight in order to remove much of the salt. Drain and discard the water.

In a large saucepan, bring to the boil enough fresh water to cover the gammon. Add the gammon joint, reduce the heat slightly and cook for approximately 15 minutes. Remove from the heat and discard the cooking water. Set aside the gammon.

Place approximately 5 litres of fresh water in a large, clean saucepan. Add the gammon, vegetables and tomatoes, making sure all the ingredients are covered with water. If not, add some more. Bring to the boil, reduce the heat and simmer for 40 minutes, skimming the top from time to time.

Remove from the heat and drain the liquid into another saucepan (you should have approximately 3.5 litres left). Taste this stock and, if necessary, adjust the seasoning by adding some salt and pepper. Place on the heat and bring to the boil, then add the spelt, gradually mixing it with a wooden spoon as you are pouring. Reduce the heat to a low setting and simmer for approximately 45 minutes or according to the instructions on the packet. Stir frequently with a wooden spoon to make sure the spelt does not stick to the bottom of the pan – if necessary, add more boiling water. The spelt should be tender when cooked.

In the meantime, if you are making a one-course dish, cut the cooked gammon into thin strips and mix it into the soup when it is ready. Serve immediately with freshly grated pecorino cheese and some freshly ground black pepper.

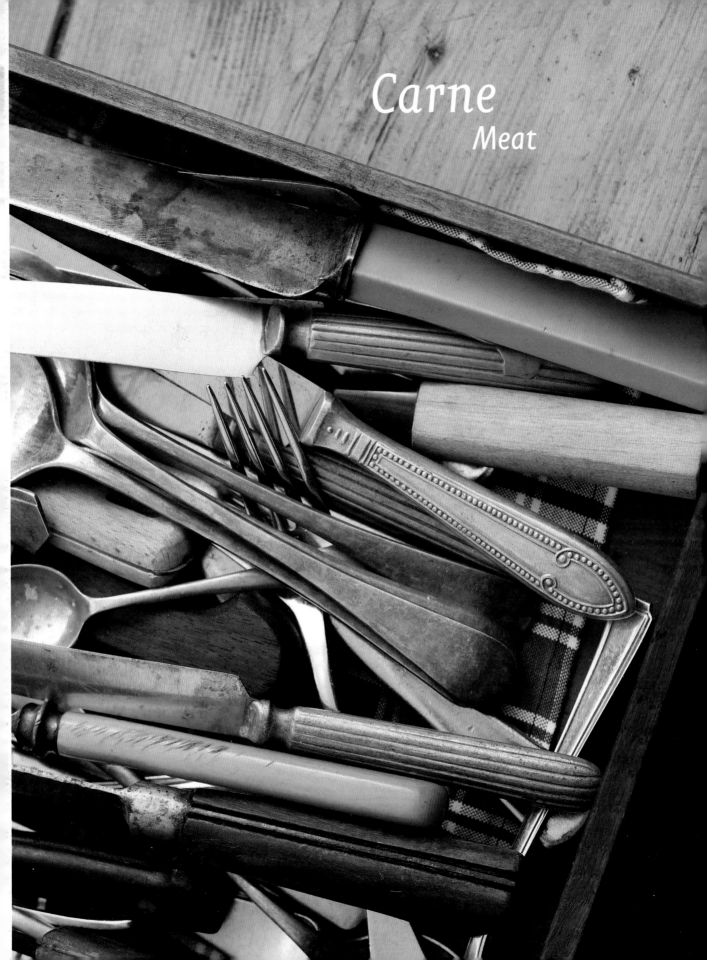

Carne
Meat

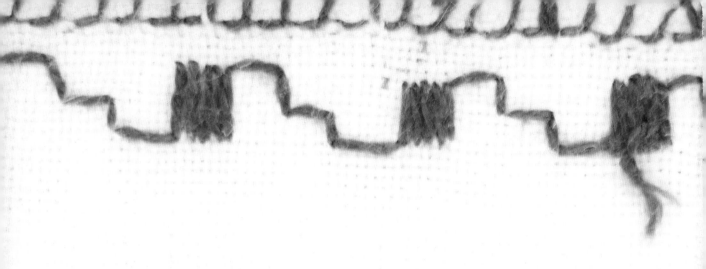

I have always considered myself lucky that I grew up in a time when meat came from local farmers, chickens ran around free-range in our backyard and game was shot by my father and his friends. We may not have consumed an enormous amount of meat, but what we did eat was genuine and organic. I also learnt about the different parts of the animal and its butchering and I knew immediately if the cut was good or bad. No one was squeamish about killing an animal for food, nor about the huge carcasses in full view at the butcher's or feathers scattered around our yard or kitchen.

Butchers in those days bought live cows directly from the farmers who raised them. They would go and get them and then the cow would walk at the head of what seemed like a procession to the slaughter, with the butcher beside and his assistant behind. My little sister often tagged along at the end of the procession because she wanted to console the cow, which always made me laugh! It has never deterred her from eating meat though, especially beef – one of her favourite foods. I'm sure it helped that during important family occasions, my grandfather and father were in charge of carving meat once it was cooked and they always saved the most tender succulent pieces for the children.

Our meat was always full of flavour and needed little seasoning. I always remember the wonderful freshly made beef stock which would bubble in the big pot in the kitchen. The beef was given to us by a friend of my mother, whose husband was a farmer and butcher, so we had the tenderest meat. Together with celery, potatoes, onions, tomatoes and a small bone or bit of sinew, everything gave off such indescribable flavours. And that little star-shaped pasta added to the broth was my favourite. To finish off, we would grate some local cheese on top. It was real comfort food and I still make it today for all the family on cold, grey days.

In Tuscany, the famous T-bone steak dish known as *Costata alla fiorentina* is one of Italy's favourites and butchers in towns and villages compete to stock the best! There are rules and regulations over the right thickness and weight and it has to be cooked in the simple, traditional way – brushed with olive oil, seared over charcoal and seasoned with salt at the end. When I visit restaurants in Tuscany, I am always amazed to see huge roasting spits laden with chicken, pork loin, goat, guinea fowl, various types of game from small birds to wild boar, all filling the restaurant with the most wonderful aroma.

Milan has given the world *Cotoletta impanatta* – veal cutlet beaten thinly, dipped in egg, coated in breadcrumbs and shallow fried – as well as *Ossobuco*, veal shin cooked in a light tomato sauce.

Then we have the Piemontese *Bollito misto*,

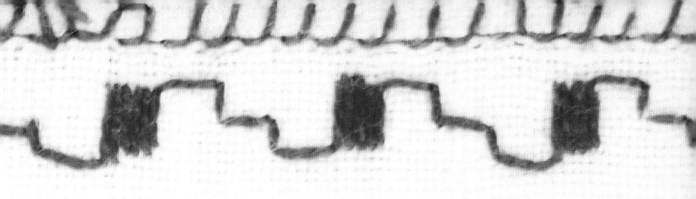

which consists of different cuts of beef, veal, chicken or capon, sausages and vegetables all boiled together. In the past, this delicious dish was served to prisoners before they faced the gallows! One of my favourite meat dishes is the Roman *porchetta*, a whole boned pig, filled with herbs, wild fennel and garlic and then roasted.

In many rural parts of Italy, the killing of the pig, usually carried out in winter months, was a very important ritual, which I remember very vividly from when I was a child. No part of the pig was ever wasted and lots of cured meats and sausages were made, which were then hung over the fireplace. The combination of warm air and smoke helped them to mature to perfection. These days, large producers have specially made rooms where this takes place. Italy is also famous for its cured meats, such as the different hams and salami, the air-dried beef *bresaola*, *zampone*, made from minced pork and spices and many others.

In Sardinia, even today, pork and lamb seasoned with herbs are roasted underground – a deep hole is dug, the meat put in a lidded pot which is covered with earth and slow-cooked by a fire on top, bringing out excellent results.

Obviously we cannot cook by digging big holes in the ground, but we can ensure that whatever meat we use is good quality by checking that the meat fibre is thin and compact and its smell fresh and pleasant.

At home, it is best not to leave meat in the fridge for too long as this mars its flavour and quality. When cooking steaks, ensure the pan is very hot so that the meat seals well and its juices do not escape. Red meat can be cooked rare and some consumed raw, such as the famous beef carpaccio.

Boiling meat is the simplest method of cooking, but to taste good it has to be cooked in large quantities with different cuts of meat. Grilled meats should be cooked over very hot coals, wood or on a griddle pan ensuring it does not catch alight as this will only burn the meat on the outside and not cook it inside. Turn the meat only once and salt it at the end.

Years ago in my village, meat was not consumed very often as we were by the sea and fish would obviously cost a lot less. I remember certain families would hide large hunks of meat under their jacket so as not to be seen to be able to afford this delicacy! Today, all this amazes me, as I watch the price of fish go higher and higher. Nowadays there is a great variety of meat on the market which unfortunately has not been reared organically like it once was, thereby making meat tough, unappetising and above all lacking in important nutrients. I believe we should only buy the good-quality, organic variety from a reliable source. If we have to reduce our weekly intake of meat to be able to afford the best, then so be it.

Spezzattino d'agnello con patate

Lamb and potato stew

This lamb stew is simple to prepare, but you will need to stay close by it because the stock needs to be added gradually, to prevent boiling the meat. The potatoes and mangetout are added later so they don't overcook, but once the potatoes are added do not stir, as this will mash them. If you prefer, you can substitute veal or beef for the lamb. A wonderful stew for all the family.

10–12 SERVINGS

1.6kg lamb, cut into small pieces

salt and pepper

a little flour, for dusting

10 tablespoons extra-virgin olive oil

3 onions, finely chopped

2 celery stalks

4 sage leaves

250g baby carrots, peeled and left whole

200ml white wine

approx. 1.2 litres hot vegetable or meat stock

1kg potatoes, peeled, washed and cut into chunks

800g mangetout, washed and left whole

Season the pieces of lamb well with salt and pepper, then dust in the flour, mixing the meat well with your hands and shaking off the excess. Set aside.

In a large, deep frying pan, heat the olive oil and add the onions, celery, sage leaves and carrots. Stir-fry on a medium heat until the onion and celery soften, stirring from time to time to avoid any vegetables burning and sticking.

Add the meat and seal on all sides. Add the wine and boil until the liquid evaporates. Reduce the heat, cover the pan with a lid and cook on a medium heat for 5 minutes. Remove the lid and pour in a couple of ladlefuls of stock and continue to cook on a medium heat for 40 minutes, adding more stock if necessary.

Stir in the potatoes, with some more stock if necessary, cover with a lid and cook for 20 minutes. Five minutes before the end of the cooking time, gently stir in the mangetout, making sure the potatoes don't break up. Season to taste, if necessary. Remove from the heat and serve.

Cosciotto d'agnello limonato al cartoccio

Foil-wrapped leg of lamb baked with lemon

This is a family recipe that was often cooked at springtime when the baby lambs were born and at their best to eat. A leg was simply roasted in our wood-fired oven together with our locally grown lemons and rosemary, and the smell emanating from our kitchen was intoxicating! Wrapping the lamb in foil keeps it moist during cooking, as well as keeping all the wonderful flavours together. Simple to prepare, this makes a great Sunday lunch!

8 SERVINGS

1.6kg leg of lamb (or 2 smaller legs)

salt and pepper, to taste

3 sprigs of rosemary

8 tablespoons extra-virgin olive oil

4 lemons, sliced

Preheat the oven to 180°C/350°F/gas 4.

Rub the lamb all over with salt, pepper and the sprigs of rosemary. Heat the extra-virgin olive oil in a large saucepan and place the lamb in it, sealing the meat all over. Remove from the heat and set aside. Line an ovenproof dish with lots of foil, topped with some greaseproof paper to prevent the lamb from sticking. Place the lamb in the lined dish and cover it with lemon slices. Wrap up the meat with the excess foil, keeping it a little loose.

Place the lamb in the preheated oven and roast for 1 hour and 20 minutes or until the lamb is cooked. Remove from the oven and leave the meat to rest for 10–15 minutes before serving. Remove the foil and greaseproof papers, carefully pouring any juices left in the foil all over the cooked lamb.

Bistecche alla pizzaiola

Sirloin steaks in a tomato and caper sauce

This simple and quick, tangy sauce livens up sirloin steaks and is very typical of Southern Italy, with its mouthwatering tomatoes, capers and home-dried oregano. It is delicious as a midweek supper served with rice or couscous or just good bread to mop up the sauce. If you have leftover tomato sauce, you could use it on pasta or on bruschetta the next day.

8 SERVINGS

6 tablespoons extra-virgin olive oil

8 sirloin steaks, thinly cut (weighing approx. 150g each)

2 garlic cloves, thinly sliced

6 anchovy fillets

2 tablespoons capers, washed and dried

a handful of fresh parsley, finely chopped

500g tinned plum tomatoes, finely chopped (or use fresh plum or cherry tomatoes when in season, deseeded and finely chopped)

2 teaspoons dried oregano

salt and pepper, to taste (optional)

In a large, shallow frying pan, heat the olive oil and fry the steaks on both sides to seal the meat. Remove the meat from the pan and set aside. Using the same frying pan, stir-fry the garlic, anchovies, capers and half of the parsley for 2–3 minutes. Add the tomatoes and oregano and cook on a high heat for one minute, stirring well.

Lower the heat and add the steaks, making sure they are covered with the tomato sauce, and cook for about 10–15 minutes, depending on the thickness of the meat. Check for seasoning and if necessary add some salt and pepper.

Remove from the heat, sprinkle with the remaining parsley and serve immediately.

Brasato

Beef braised in red wine

This is a really simple recipe that is perfect for feeding lots of people. Due to the slow cooking of the beef, it melts in your mouth it is so tender! Delicious served with a purée of root vegetables such as carrot and celeriac. If you prefer, you can substitute vegetable stock for half the wine.

8 SERVINGS

salt and pepper

2kg beef topside

12 tablespoons olive oil

3 onions, finely chopped

6 carrots, finely chopped

8 celery sticks, finely chopped

4 sprigs of rosemary

4 garlic cloves, finely chopped

2 litres red wine

Rub a little salt and pepper all over the meat. Heat the olive oil in a large saucepan and, when hot, add the meat and seal well all over. Remove and set aside.

In the same saucepan, add the chopped onions, carrots, celery, rosemary and garlic and sweat for a couple of minutes. Discard the rosemary, return the meat to the pan and stir-fry until the meat is heated through. Add one glass of wine and cook for 1 minute. Then add the remaining wine, cover with a lid and cook on a low heat for approximately 2 hours or until the meat is tender and liquid has reduced.

Remove the meat, carve it and place the slices on a serving dish together with the vegetables and sauce.

Faraona al capuccio rosso con mela

Guinea fowl with apple and red cabbage

A lovely winter dish, this is quick and easy to prepare and perfect for serving during the Christmas period. Guinea fowl are available at good butchers' and some supermarkets, but if you prefer, you can use capon or turkey pieces.

8–12 SERVINGS

2 medium-sized guinea fowl, cut into 12 pieces (ask your butcher to do this or buy ready-cut pieces)

salt and pepper

12 strips of pancetta, left whole

16 tablespoons extra-virgin olive oil

150g pancetta, finely chopped

6 cloves

5 Golden Delicious apples, peeled, cored and cubed

2 medium-sized red cabbages, finely chopped into strips

Preheat the oven to 240°C/465°F/gas 9.

Season each piece of guinea fowl with salt and pepper and wrap them individually in a strip of pancetta. Place in an ovenproof dish, drizzle with about 6 tablespoons of the olive oil, reduce the oven temperature to 200°C/400°F/gas 6 and bake in the oven for 30 minutes. Turn the pieces over halfway through cooking.

In a large saucepan, heat the remaining olive oil and stir-fry the finely chopped pancetta. Add the cloves, apples and cabbages and season with salt and pepper. Cover with a lid and cook on a medium heat for 40 minutes, checking and stirring from time to time and adding a little boiling water, if necessary.

Remove the guinea fowl pieces from the oven and tip them into the pan with the cabbage mixture, including the pan juices. Cook for a further 5 minutes. Serve immediately with perhaps some roast potatoes.

Cotolettine alle noci

Pork slices coated in walnuts and breadcrumbs

Breadcrumbed pork loin slices are very popular in Italy and the same recipe is also used for veal or pounded chicken breasts. All these variations are extremely popular with children who won't usually eat meat, but if they need a little more encouragement you can serve this with my *Herby Chips* (see page 133). These breadcrumbed slices can be prepared the day before and fried just before lunch or dinner. Any leftovers can be eaten cold in a sandwich or reheated under the grill. The addition of walnuts to the breadcrumb coating gives the crust a lovely crunchy texture and combines very well with pork meat, as well as being healthy.

8 SERVINGS

100g shelled walnuts, very finely chopped (or use a food processor)

3 slices of white bread, very finely chopped (or use a food processor)

home-made or natural breadcrumbs (as required)

5 sprigs of thyme, leaves stripped and stem discarded

salt and pepper, to taste

8 slices of pork loin, thinly cut to approx. ½cm

plain flour, for dusting

3 eggs, beaten

10 tablespoons olive oil

lemon wedges, to serve

Mix together the walnuts, bread, breadcrumbs, thyme and salt and pepper on a plate.

Dust the pork loin slices in flour, shaking off the excess, then dip them into the beaten egg, followed by the walnut and bread mix. Press the slices down well with your hands to coat them in as much of the mixture as possible.

In a large, non-stick frying pan, heat the olive oil and fry the pork slices for about 4–5 minutes on each side or until well cooked on the inside. Serve with lemon wedges, if desired, and a nice crunchy salad.

Pollo ripieno e bolitto

Boiled stuffed chicken

This is a very traditional recipe made throughout Italy, especially during the Christmas season. I love boiled chicken, which has to be a truly organic one, and the taste of the broth which comes from it is wonderful. The chicken and its broth is highly nutritious and perfect for all the family. The broth can be made into *Eggy Soup*, see recipe on page 35. Or you can add some small pasta shapes, *pastina* (my girls love the little stars and the alphabet and numbers) or for a more substantial soup, add some small meat-filled tortellini or raviolini, easily obtainable from delis and supermarkets.

8 SERVINGS

3 slices of white bread

approx. 250ml milk (you may need a little less or more)

200g minced beef

200g minced pork

1 garlic clove, finely chopped

2 eggs

salt and pepper, to taste

a handful of fresh parsley, finely chopped

1 large, free-range, organic chicken, including its livers

1 egg, hard-boiled and peeled

1 large carrot, peeled and left whole

2 celery stalks, cut in half

1 leek, left whole

1 large onion, peeled and left whole

toothpicks or needle and thread for sealing the chicken

Soak the bread in the milk then press the bread well between your hands to drain off the excess milk. Set aside.

In a large bowl, place the minced meats, bread, garlic, raw eggs, salt, pepper and parsley and mix well together. Stuff the chicken with this mixture, followed by the boiled egg. Seal well either with toothpicks or using a needle and thread – you must make sure that the stuffing does not escape during cooking.

Place the stuffed chicken in a large saucepan together with the carrot, celery, leek, onion, salt and a little pepper. Cover with lots of cold water to at least 10cm above the chicken. Cover with a lid, bring to the boil, then lower the heat and let the chicken simmer gently for approximately one and a half hours or until the chicken is cooked through and a nice broth is obtained.

Carefully remove the chicken from the pan and place it on a board. Drain the vegetables and discard them, reserving the broth. (You can make a lovely *stracciatella* with the broth, see page 35.)

To serve the chicken: remove the toothpicks or cut the thread then slice up the chicken before serving it with some of the stuffing. And don't forget the egg!

Fegato con cipollotti

Calf's liver with large spring onions

Easy and simple to make, this is my version of the classic *Fegato alla Veneziana* that is popular throughout Italy and in many Italian restaurants abroad. This was also a favourite family dish which my mother often cooked for us. She always added bay leaves to give it flavour and wine vinegar, which gave off a wonderful aroma whilst cooking. I have used *cipollotti* here (which are very large spring onions), as they are fresher, tender and less sharp than ordinary onions. They are obtainable from good greengrocers or farmers' markets – look out for them. Obviously, if you can't find them then normal white onions will suffice. This is delicious served with some steamed vegetables and lots of good bread to mop up the sauce.

8 SERVINGS

8 tablespoons extra-virgin olive oil

30g butter

3 bay leaves

700g large spring onions, sliced in half

1kg calf's liver, thinly sliced

plain flour, for coating

4 tablespoons red or white wine vinegar

salt and pepper, to taste

Heat the olive oil and butter in a large frying pan. Add the bay leaves and allow their flavour to infuse for a minute. Reduce the heat, add the onions, cover with a lid and cook for about 20 minutes or until soft and golden in colour – make sure you do not burn them. Remove and set aside.

Coat the calf's liver very lightly in flour, shaking off the excess. Increase the heat and place in the frying pan. Fry on both sides for about 2–3 minutes. Reduce the heat and add the cooked onions, stirring well. Increase the heat and, whilst stirring, add the vinegar and cook for a further 2 minutes until well absorbed and you obtain a creamy consistency. Add salt and pepper to taste and serve immediately.

Tip: **Don't overcook the liver, otherwise it will become hard.**

Coda di bue alla vaccinara con sedano

Braised oxtail with celery

This traditional Roman recipe is extremely easy to prepare, but it does take a long time to cook as the oxtail has to be really tender. When I first came to England, oxtail was very popular and everyone made soup with it. Nowadays it is not so common, but I really wanted to include this recipe. Oxtail and pork make a great combination, and the pork does give the dish a real kick! The celery is added at the end to bring freshness to this rich dish.

This can be made a couple of days in advance – which not only saves time on the day it is needed, but also helps the flavours to develop even more. Serve with lots of lovely bread and a good glass of red wine – Italian, of course!

8 SERVINGS

2kg oxtail (ask your butcher to cut this into chunks – aim for 2 chunks per person)

salt and pepper, to taste

8 tablespoons extra-virgin olive oil

3 onions, finely chopped

4 carrots, finely chopped

2 garlic cloves, left whole

3 bay leaves

a handful of parsley, finely chopped

500g piece of pancetta, cut into ½cm slices (or use pork belly)

3 tablespoons white wine vinegar

400ml red wine

6 tablespoons tomato passata

approx. 1.5 litres vegetable stock

4 stalks celery, roughly chopped

Place the pieces of oxtail in cold water, rinse well and pat dry with kitchen towel. Season with a little salt and pepper. Set aside.

In a large saucepan, heat the olive oil. Add the onions, carrots, garlic, bay leaves and parsley and cook until all the vegetables soften. Add the oxtail and pancetta and seal the meat well on all sides. Add the vinegar and cook for 1 minute. Add the wine and allow it to evaporate, then add the tomato passata and the stock. Reduce the heat, cover with a lid and cook for approximately 2½–3 hours or until the meat is tender. During cooking, check the meat from time to time to make sure it does not stick to the bottom of the pan.

Meanwhile, in a separate saucepan, boil the celery until tender. Drain, then add to the meat at the end of cooking time. Increase the heat and cook on a high heat for a further 5 minutes or until the liquid has reduced and the sauce thickened. Remove from the heat and serve.

Tip: You could make this a two-course dish: serve the sauce with some pasta, such as penne rigatoni, topped with some grated pecorino or Parmesan cheese as a first course; then serve the meat as a main course with some steamed vegetables.

Ossobuco
Veal shins with lemon and parsley

My version of this tasty Milanese classic is extremely easy to prepare. It is traditionally served with saffron risotto, which is equally simple to make: all you need to do is make a basic risotto with a little onion, then at the end stir in a few strands of saffron before finishing off with butter and Parmesan. Serve the risotto on individual plates and top with one veal shin per person and pour over the sauce.

This is a rich, nutritious dish and perfect for a winter get-together with lots of family and friends. Most butchers stock veal shins, but if you can't find them you can replace with lamb shanks. The finely chopped gremolada mixture adds extra flavour to the sauce.

10 SERVINGS

10 veal shins, cut into approx. 5cm pieces (ask your butcher to do this)

plain flour, for coating

150g butter

salt and pepper, to taste

1 glass white wine

2 medium-sized onions, finely chopped

3 carrots, finely chopped

400g tomato passata

500ml vegetable stock

FOR THE GREMOLADA

2 garlic cloves, finely chopped

zest of 1 lemon

a handful of fresh parsley, finely chopped

2 anchovies, finely chopped

Coat the veal shins all over with the plain flour. On a high heat, melt the butter in a casserole dish that is large enough to hold all the shins in one layer. Add salt and pepper and seal the meat well on all sides. Add the wine and allow it to evaporate by half. Remove the meat and set aside.

Add the onions and carrots to the pan and cook on a high heat for about 5 minutes until the remaining wine evaporates and the onions and carrots have softened. Return the meat to the pan. Add the tomato passata and the vegetable stock, reduce the heat to medium, cover with a lid and cook for about an hour until the meat is cooked through and the sauce has thickened. Check from time to time and don't allow it to dry out – add more vegetable stock if necessary. Halfway through cooking, carefully turn over the shins. At the end of cooking, increase the heat and cook on high for a couple of minutes to thicken the sauce.

Meanwhile, make the gremolada: chop all the ingredients very finely using a mezzaluna (if you have one) or a sharp knife and set aside.

When the veal shins are cooked, remove them and place on a large serving dish. Add the gremolada to the sauce in the pan and mix together well. Pour the sauce over the meat and serve immediately with saffron risotto.

Lepre con patate e mele al limone

Hare with potatoes, apples and lemon

It was always a feast when my father brought home hare, which we usually cooked very simply with some potatoes. As hare has quite a gamey taste, we would put it in cold water and change the water frequently throughout the day to clean it. (You don't have to do this if you buy your hare from the butcher, but if you happen to shoot one yourself or are given a wild one, I suggest you do this.) I have added apples and lemon juice to this dish to give it a slightly sweet and sour taste, which works really well with game. If you can't find hare, you can replace with rabbit.

10 SERVINGS

5 apples, cored and cut into thick rings

juice of 2 large lemons

2.5kg hare chunks

salt and pepper, to taste

10 tablespoons extra-virgin olive oil

5 sprigs of rosemary

2 glasses white wine

1 litre beef stock

6 large potatoes, peeled and cut into thick rounds

100g butter

Place the apple rings in the lemon juice and set aside.

Season the hare chunks with salt and pepper. Heat the olive oil in a large frying pan, add the hare chunks with the rosemary and seal the meat well on all sides. Add the wine and stock and reduce the heat. Cover with a lid and simmer gently for 1 hour or until the hare is tender and cooked. Halfway through cooking, add the potatoes and the lemon juice from the apples – but don't add the apples yet.

In the meantime, melt the butter in a frying pan, add the apples and caramelise them on all sides.

Serve the hare in all its juices alongside the potatoes and apples.

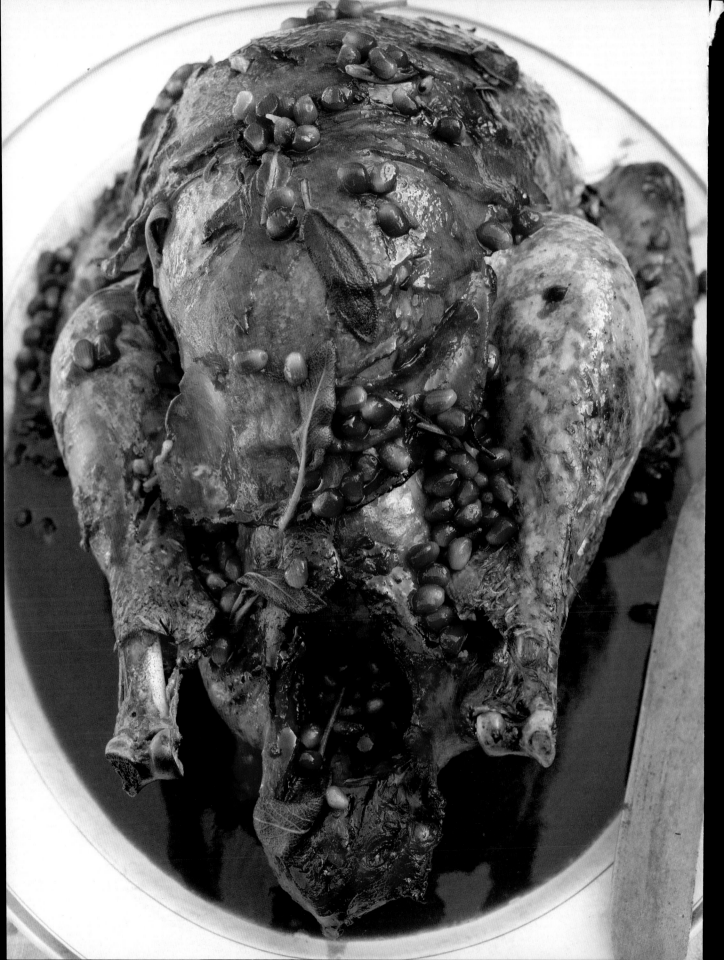

Tacchino arrosto con il melograno e arancia

Turkey roasted with pomegranate and orange

This is a light roast turkey dish that can easily be eaten in the middle of summer as well as at Christmas time. Pomegranate juice is now widely available all year round, so you can use that instead of juicing fresh pomegranates; however, I still prefer the juice of freshly squeezed fruit. Pomegranates and oranges go really well together and give a delicious tangy flavour to the turkey. The dish is very simple to make and is perfect served to a large group of people, accompanied by roast potatoes and steamed vegetables.

12 SERVINGS

100g butter

salt and pepper, to taste

2 oranges, peel and pith removed, but left whole

1 free-range, organic turkey (weighing approx. 3kg)

200g sliced pancetta

500ml stock

200ml white wine

juice of 4 pomegranates (or 300ml pomegranate juice)

FOR THE SAUCE

2 oranges, roughly chopped into pieces with the skin on

100g unsalted butter

3 sage leaves

1 glass white wine

6 tablespoons pomegranate juice

seeds of 1 pomegranate

salt and pepper, to taste

Preheat the oven to 240°C/465°F/gas 9.

Stuff half the butter, a little salt and the oranges into the cavity of the turkey. Gently open up the skin of the breast and rub in salt, pepper and butter. Do the same over the whole turkey. Drape the slices of pancetta over the turkey, place in an ovenproof dish, pour in the stock and wine, and cover with foil. Reduce the oven to 180°C/350°F/gas 4 and place the turkey in the oven, basting from time to time. After and hour and a half, remove the turkey, pour over the pomegranate juice and season with a little salt and pepper. Recover with the foil, return to the oven and continue to cook for a further hour. Remove the foil and continue to roast for half an hour until the turkey is cooked through.

Take the turkey out of the oven and remove the oranges from the cavity. Cover the turkey with foil and leave it to rest.

To make the sauce: roughly chop the cooked and uncooked oranges and set aside. Melt the butter in a small pan, add the sage leaves and leave to infuse (on the heat) for a minute, then add the chopped oranges and allow them to release their flavour for a minute or so. Add the wine and allow it to evaporate. Add the pomegranate juice, pomegranate seeds, salt and pepper and cook for 3 or 4 minutes until you obtain a smooth sauce.

Carve the turkey and serve the slices with the pomegranate and orange sauce.

Pesce
Fish

As a country surrounded on three sides by the sea, Italy has always been a fishing nation. The combination of many fish species swimming in its crystalline waters, its pristine forests untouched by man and its long culinary history have contributed to the creation of a national seafood cuisine that is both rich and ingenious. (Stimulated in no small measure, of course, by the Catholic tradition of eating fish on Friday.)

However, while the variety of seafood is great, the number of ways in which it is prepared are few, because Italians prefer simple methods of cooking which leave the individual flavour of each fish to speak for itself. The important thing is that the fish is as fresh as possible, both to maintain its flavour and preserve its nutritional value. I was born beside the sea, so I have always found it easy to judge how fresh a fish is: the eyes should be bright and clear, the gills still coloured red with blood, and when you bring your nose up close to it you should be able to smell the sea or the river – never an unpleasant odour.

When I was a child, my mother made me eat fish eyes, which when cooked became little hard, white balls, full of phosphorus. She said this was a nutrient that helped develop intelligence! In my travels throughout Italy and here in England, I am always fascinated by the sight of the fishmonger's table piled high with fish ready for sale. Proud swordfish sit next to happier-looking red mullet, stern crabs cohabit with sardines and anchovies, sea-snails grip the side of the bucket with their suckers, clams splash about in the water, octopus both great and small brood away in buckets of seawater and vainly attempt the great escape up the impossible walls of their containers, and the moist flesh of fresh tuna waits to be sliced up just at the moment of sale. It is as if a great chunk of the sea has been lifted straight up and plopped down onto the table – as indeed it has.

Where I grew up, the fishmonger, especially when speaking with a foreigner who might perhaps be shopping with the help of a local housewife, would provide meticulous instructions for how to prepare each type of fish he sold you: how to fry it or boil it, how to marinate it and how to eat it raw. And he would do this with such pride and passion that you would think he had gone out and caught every fish himself! Best of all, he would remind you that sitting under a pergola by the sea with a plate of fried fish and a glass of good wine in your hand was an experience that you would remember for the rest of your life.

Despite the abundance of native fish varieties, Italians also import fish from abroad – most notably cod, which is either preserved in salt (such as *baccalà*) or air-dried (*stoccafisso*). Both have a quite distinct flavour and are utterly delicious. Whether boiled or fried, when served with potatoes, olives, cherry tomatoes and parsley, these dishes are family favourites on every table. In Southern Italy anchovies preserved in salt are very popular; they are left for about one year in the salt, then filleted when required. The flesh is pink in colour and gives off a wonderful scent and the juice that oozes from the salt-packed anchovies is filtered and used to dress spaghetti. Simply delicious!

Tuna is mainly caught off the coasts of Sicily and is served grilled, fried, baked in the oven or preserved, and it can easily take the place of a beef steak. Farmed fish such as *spigola* (seabass), *orata* (bream) and *sarago* (white bream) are also excellent.

In Italian restaurants nowadays the types of fish being served are put on display for customers to see when they walk in, but this was not always the case. Up until a few years ago, seaside restaurants kept their fish out of view, swimming in nets in the sea below, which their chefs would pull up to get fresh fish dishes as needed. These places were real culinary aquariums!

My mother had relatives living close to the port in the nearby town of Castellamare di Stabia, on the Bay of Naples, where there was, and still is, a natural spring that flows directly into the sea. Its waters had curative powers and my task was to fill up large bottles with it and bring them home. It was a job I really liked because close by you could find a number of cooking sheds where they sold freshly cooked mussels, razor clams, sea urchins and all manner of grilled fish, all plucked straight from their holding nets just before going on the stove. The shed that fascinated me the most was the one where they sold octopus and mussels. The stalls were painted in bright colours, displaying copper amphoras covered in brightly coloured paper. In the centre was a huge copper pot where they cooked enormous octopuses simply in seawater to produce a broth that was served in bowls sprinkled with black pepper and freshly squeezed lemon juice.

Nowadays, mussels and razor clams are rarely eaten because of concerns about pollution, but the flavour of fresh sea urchins, split open and with lemon juice squeezed over it, is hard to forget. That slippery flesh sliding down your throat leaves such a fantastic taste on your palate.

The old fishermen knew exactly where to fish. They all had their secret spots where the fish ran thick and they kept their secrets as tightly as truffle-hunters keep theirs. But they trusted me, and when I used to help them sew their nets they could speak freely, because they knew that I was not going to be a fisherman. Although, to be honest, I was, and still am, strongly drawn to the sea.

Even now, when I return to Italy I still stare out to sea in the evening, wondering who might be in the small fishing boats with their lights gleaming on the water far off from shore.

They are not as common as they used to be, but the sight of these boats, if you have the chance to see them, is pure magic. They are like stars dancing on the surface of the water in slow rhythm with the waves as the moon sends down its soft glow, while the sea speaks to you in its own language with each wave that arrives on shore. Time seems to stand still then, and you drift far, far away!

Millefoglie di merluzzo e patate

Layered hake and potato bake

When I first made this dish, I used raw potatoes and raw fish and baked them with the rest of the ingredients. However, now I prefer to bake the potatoes first to get them nice and crispy. It takes a little more time, but it is definitely well worth the effort and it makes it look lovely, too, when served. When cooking the fish and adding the condiments (butter, extra-virgin olive oil and lemon juice), make sure the fish is dry, otherwise the crispy potatoes will go soggy. If you prefer, you can substitute cod for the hake.

8–10 SERVINGS

1kg hake fillets (or cod)

2 garlic cloves

500ml milk

3 bay leaves

salt and pepper, to taste

7 medium-sized potatoes

200ml extra-virgin olive oil, plus extra for drizzling

60g butter

juice of 2 lemons, strained through a sieve

Preheat the oven to 180°C/350°F/gas 4.

In a saucepan large enough to hold the fish, place the hake, garlic, milk, bay leaves and some salt and pepper. Bring to the boil, then lower the heat and simmer gently for 10–15 minutes or until the fish is cooked and the milk has been absorbed.

Meanwhile, thinly slice the potatoes in rounds approximately 5mm thick. Place them on a large, lightly greased baking tray. Drizzle some olive oil and sprinkle some salt over the top of the potatoes and place them in the preheated oven for 20 minutes or until they are golden brown. Remove and set aside, but leave the oven on.

In a small pan, melt the butter then tip it over the fish. Pour over the olive oil and lemon juice. Mix well together, flaking the fish with a fork.

Line a large ovenproof dish with a layer of the potatoes, then add a layer of fish, followed by another of potatoes, then fish, and continue in this way until you have finished all the fish and end up with a layer of potatoes on the top. Place the dish in the oven for approximately 5–10 minutes or until heated through. Serve immediately.

Orata ai fiori di cappero con zucchini e cipolle

Fillets of sea bream with a caper and lemon sauce served with roasted vegetables

Sea bream is a tasty white fish whose fillets are boneless and easy to cook. I have combined these fish fillets with a sauce of tangy capers and lemon juice. The large capers are obtainable in good delis, but if you can't find them the small ones will suffice, preserved either under salt or in brine. If they are preserved under salt, you will have to rinse them well before use. I have not added salt to the sauce as the capers are quite salty, but feel free to add extra if you wish.

This is a quick and easy dish to prepare and lovely for a main course dinner party. The roasted courgettes and onions are a perfect side dish and also extremely simple to prepare.

8 SERVINGS

120g butter

100g large capers, cut in half (or if using small ones, leave whole)

juice of 2 large, unwaxed lemons

a handful of chives, finely chopped

8 bream fillets, weighing 200g each

plain flour, for coating

FOR THE ROASTED VEGETABLES

6 courgettes, roughly chopped into batons

4 small onions, chopped into segments

10 tablespoons extra-virgin olive oil

2 sprigs of thyme

2 sprigs of rosemary

2 garlic cloves, cut in half

salt and pepper, to taste

Preheat the oven to 200°C/400°F/gas 6.

First, prepare the vegetables. Place the courgettes and onions in an ovenproof dish. Drizzle with the olive oil and sprinkle with the thyme, rosemary, garlic and salt and pepper. Place in the oven for approximately 20 minutes or until they are tender.

Meanwhile, heat 60g of the butter in a large frying pan, add the capers and stir-fry for about 3 minutes over a medium heat. Add the lemon juice and chives and stir-fry for a further 3 or 4 minutes. Turn off the heat and set aside.

Coat the bream fillets in the flour, shaking off any excess. Heat the remaining butter in another frying pan and fry the fillets on both sides for a couple of minutes or until cooked through and golden. Remove and dry on kitchen towel. When all the fillets are cooked, heat through the caper sauce and add the bream fillets to it. Cook for a further 2 minutes, then serve immediately with the roasted vegetables.

Sogliola al prosciutto crudo in salsa d'alloro

Fillets of sole wrapped in Parma ham in a bay leaf sauce

Sole fillets marry very well with Parma ham, and combining both with this simple sauce of shallots and bay leaves makes this a lovely main course dish. For guests who don't eat meat, simply bake, grill or poach the fish without the Parma ham and serve with the sauce. Delicious accompanied by boiled baby potatoes.

8 SERVINGS

16 slices of Parma ham

16 fillets of sole, weighing approx. 100g each (or 8 fillets of sole, weighing approx. 200g each and cut in half lengthways)

16 small sprigs of parsley

salt and pepper, to taste

16 chive leaves (for tying up the fillets)

greaseproof paper

FOR THE PASTE

35g capers

½ garlic clove, finely chopped

2 tablespoons extra-virgin olive oil

FOR THE SAUCE

8 tablespoons extra-virgin olive oil

12 bay leaves, finely chopped

2 shallots, finely chopped

2 garlic cloves, finely chopped

2 handfuls of fresh parsley, finely chopped

400ml white wine blended with 1 teaspoon cornflour

salt and pepper, to taste

Preheat the oven to 200°C/400°F/gas 6.

Place the capers, garlic and olive oil in a mortar and grind with a pestle until you obtain a paste.

On a clean board or work surface, line up the slices of Parma ham, place one sole fillet on each slice, very lightly brush with the caper paste, then top with a sprig of parsley. Season with salt and pepper. Carefully roll up each fillet in the ham slice and tie using a chive leaf. Line a baking tray or an ovenproof dish with greaseproof paper and place the wrapped and rolled fish fillets on it. Bake in the oven for approximately 10–15 minutes or until the fish is cooked through.

Meanwhile, make the sauce. Heat the olive oil in a small frying pan then add the bay leaves, shallots, garlic and parsley and cook on a medium heat for about 7 minutes or until the shallots have softened. Add the cornflour and wine mixture to the herbs in the pan. Stir well, add salt and pepper to taste and cook for a further 5 minutes or until the sauce has thickened.

Remove the sole fillets from the oven and transfer them to a large serving dish, or onto individual plates, and pour over the sauce before serving.

Calamari in umido

Stewed squid

Although it was my father who was the official cook in our house, there were certain dishes that my mother cooked. My mother worried whenever I went fishing, but if I told her I was going to the rocks to catch squid, she would get very excited and tell me to bring lots home. So off I would go, armed with my home-made harpoon and fishing line. My mother would wait for me, and when she saw the bucket full of squid, her eyes would light up, she would take the bucket from me and go into the kitchen to prepare her special squid dish. She would start to cook immediately, so as not to lose the fresh flavour of the sea. I would join my mother in the kitchen and sit and watch her, wondering if I would cook like her when I grew up.

I still make this dish today in exactly the same way as she did, and when I do, it is as if she is watching over me and whispering, 'Be careful, not too much salt, as there is enough salt in the sea . . . !'

This is delicious served with pasta such as linguine or spaghetti, or simply served with lots of good, rustic, toasted bread topped with the squid and a drizzle of extra-virgin olive oil. *Fantastico!*

8 SERVINGS

14 tablespoons extra-virgin olive oil

12 anchovy fillets

20g capers

4 garlic cloves, finely sliced

1 small red chilli, finely chopped (optional)

2kg squid, cleaned and chopped into quarters

salt, to taste

12 tablespoons white wine

500g cherry tomatoes, chopped in half

a bunch of parsley, roughly chopped

Heat the olive oil in a saucepan on a medium heat, add the anchovies and capers and fry until the anchovies dissolve. At this stage, add the garlic and chilli, if using, and fry for a minute, taking care not to burn them. Then add the squid and a pinch of salt and stir-fry for 2–3 minutes. Add the wine and allow it to evaporate a little.

Add the cherry tomatoes and parsley, reduce the heat to low, cover the saucepan and simmer for 45 minutes.

Rotolo di merluzzo e melanzane con cipolle rosse e funghi

Roasted, aubergine-wrapped cod with red onion and baby mushrooms

8 SERVINGS

8 tablespoons extra-virgin olive oil, plus extra for greasing

300g aubergines, thinly sliced lengthways, 3mm thick (try to get the long thin variety, and make sure they are very fresh)

2 medium-sized red onions, finely sliced

400g baby button mushrooms (try to get the really small ones; if larger, cut in half)

salt and pepper, to taste

2 tablespoons sugar

4 tablespoons white wine vinegar

800g whole, skinless cod loin

juice of ½ lemon

extra-virgin olive oil, for drizzling

FOR THE PASTE

4 anchovy fillets

2 garlic cloves, finely sliced

a handful of fresh parsley, finely chopped

1 tablespoon capers

6 tablespoons extra-virgin olive oil

This dish takes a little time to prepare, but the result is well worth it! Ask your fishmonger for a piece of skinless cod loin, so it can just be wrapped in slices of aubergine without any further fuss. The only difficulty of this recipe is ensuring that the aubergine slices stay on the fish, so I have suggested you use cling film to wrap the whole thing together, as explained in the recipe. The slightly sweet and sour onions and mushrooms in the sauce complement the fish and aubergines really well. It is the perfect dish for an alternative Sunday lunch, and one that will impress your family and friends!

Preheat the oven to 200°C/400°F/gas 6.

To make the paste, blend all the ingredients together either using a pestle and mortar or whiz in a blender until smooth. Set aside.

Lightly grease a flat baking tray with some olive oil and place the aubergine slices on it. Put them in the preheated oven for 7 minutes.

In a large frying pan, heat the olive oil, add the onions and sweat them. Add the mushrooms, salt and pepper, and on a medium heat stir-fry for about 3 minutes. Stir in the sugar, followed by the vinegar and continue to cook for 3 minutes. Remove from the heat and transfer the onions, mushrooms and juices into an ovenproof dish or roasting tin.

Remove the aubergines from the oven and, when cooler, place them in a long row just overlapping each other on a slightly larger piece of cling film. Spoon half of the paste along the centre of the aubergines.

Season the fish with a little salt and some pepper and place it on top of the aubergine slices and paste. Spoon the remaining paste over the top of the fish and pour over the lemon juice. Wrap the aubergines over the fish, covering well – if you have any extra slices, use them to patch any gaps. Wrap really tightly with the cling film so that you get a compact parcel, which you roll

backwards and forwards on the work surface. This way, you have no danger of the whole thing falling apart when you move it! Place the cling-filmed fish in the centre of the dish or tin with the onions and mushrooms. With kitchen scissors, carefully cut the cling film and remove it. You should end up with an oblong, aubergine-wrapped fish parcel surrounded by vegetables. Drizzle with a little olive oil and sprinkle with a little salt.

Reduce the oven temperature to 180°C/350°F/gas 4.

Cover the dish with foil, place it in the oven and roast for 1 hour or until the fish is cooked through. Leave it to rest for 5 minutes, then carefully transfer the wrapped fish onto a large serving dish with the vegetables and pour the sauce into a small jug. Use a serrated knife to slice the wrapped fish and serve with the vegetables and a little sauce.

Seppie ripiene
Stuffed cuttlefish

Cuttlefish always remind me of my younger fishing days in Italy. I used to love catching them and bringing them home to my mother. She would carefully clean them, remove the bone and prepare lovely meals for us. We would eat cuttlefish in different ways: simply boiled and dressed with extra-virgin olive oil, lemon juice and parsley, or in a tomato sauce accompanied by pasta, or as a main course, filled with leftover vegetables.

Ask your fishmonger for fresh cuttlefish, otherwise you can easily buy them frozen. Also, if it is not porcini season, you can use normal field mushrooms. This dish makes a delicious light meal that doesn't need any accompaniments, except a green salad, if you wish.

8 SERVINGS

8 large, whole cuttlefish (including the tentacles)

2 small onions, finely chopped (leave one slice whole)

10 tablespoons extra-virgin olive oil

2 garlic cloves, finely chopped

200g porcini mushrooms, sliced

700g potatoes, cut into small cubes

salt and pepper, to taste

½ glass white wine

6 tablespoons extra-virgin olive oil

a handful of fresh parsley, finely chopped

Thoroughly clean the cuttlefish. If you prefer, ask your fishmonger to do this, making sure you end up with 8 perfect, sack-like cuttlefish ready to fill, together with their tentacles.

Remove the tentacles from each cuttlefish – this can easily be done with kitchen scissors. Roughly chop four of them and leave the other four intact. In a large saucepan, place all the cuttlefish together with the whole and chopped tentacles and the slice of onion. Cover with cold water and boil for 5 minutes. Remove the cuttlefish sacks and set aside. Continue to cook the tentacles (which are much tougher) for 15–20 minutes or until tender.

Heat the 10 tablespoons of olive oil in a pan, add the garlic cloves and stir-fry for a minute. Then add the mushrooms and potatoes and salt and pepper. Pour in the wine and allow it to evaporate. Continue cooking on a medium heat for 10 minutes, then add the chopped and whole tentacles. Mix well together and remove from the heat. Remove the whole tentacles and set aside.

Preheat the oven to 200°C/400°F/gas 6.

Fill each cuttlefish with the potato and mushroom mixture, making sure you drain off any excess olive oil.

Drizzle an ovenproof dish with the 6 tablespoons of olive oil then drop on it the finely chopped onions and any leftover filling mixture (including any excess olive oil). Place the filled cuttlefish with the four whole tentacles on the tray and sprinkle with half of the chopped parsley. Bake in the oven for about 15–20 minutes. Remove, sprinkle with the remaining parsley and serve.

Tonno alla griglia

Grilled tuna with tomatoes and sweet red onions

Tuna is widely eaten in Mediterranean countries, both in its preserved and fresh form. This fish has a dark red flesh with an intense flavour and is highly nutritious. It can be eaten raw as a carpaccio, and the very expensive *bottarga* is made from its eggs, which is used in many fine restaurants grated over pasta or fish dishes.

This light, fresh recipe is very simple to prepare, but please make sure that you use good-quality ingredients. Don't be afraid to ask your fishmonger for the freshest tuna, and do buy the best tomatoes you can find.

12 SERVINGS

salt and pepper

2.5kg tuna, cut into 12 slices (you may get more slices, depending on the piece of tuna you buy)

1 wine glass, approx. 250ml, extra-virgin olive oil

10 ripe plum tomatoes (or tomatoes on the vine)

2 medium-sized red onions

2 garlic cloves, whole

TO GARNISH

a handful of fresh parsley, finely chopped

a few thin slices of red onion

some capers

Rub salt and pepper all over the tuna steaks, place them in a dish and cover them with the olive oil. Leave them to marinate for 30 minutes.

Meanwhile, blanch the tomatoes in boiling water for a minute, drain and remove the skins, deseed them and cut into slices. Slice the onions into rounds.

In a pan, heat the olive oil from the marinade, add the garlic and stir-fry until soft and golden, then remove and discard. Add the onion and stir-fry until soft and golden. Add the tomatoes, salt and pepper and gently stir-fry on a medium heat for 8 minutes.

Heat a griddle pan and cook the tuna steaks on each side for 4–5 minutes or until the fish is cooked through.

Heat through the tomato and onion sauce and serve with the tuna steaks. Garnish with freshly chopped parsley, some raw onion and a few capers.

Pescatrice alle erbe

Monkfish with herbs

This delicate fish is becoming more and more popular in Britain and is no longer just served in restaurants, as it once was. It is easily obtainable from your local fishmonger as well as from some supermarkets. In this simple dish the monkfish is cut into chunks and placed in a marinade of herbs and lemon, giving the fish a lot of flavour. If you have time, you can marinate the fish for longer, but if you do, place it in the fridge as you do so. This dish is delicious served with steamed fresh peas, if in season, and baby carrots.

8 SERVINGS

1.5kg monkfish, sliced in 8 pieces (ask your fishmonger to do this)

150g butter

30g capers

5 anchovy fillets, finely chopped

salt and black pepper

FOR THE MARINADE

10ml extra-virgin olive oil

1 medium-sized onion, finely chopped

10 tablespoons white wine

juice of 2 large lemons

2 handfuls of fresh parsley, finely chopped

5 sprigs of thyme

Rinse the fish under cold running water, then pat dry with clean kitchen towel.

First make the marinade: mix all the ingredients together, then pour over the fish and leave to marinate for about 20 minutes, turning the fish halfway through.

Drain the marinade from the monkfish and reserve it. Heat the butter in a large pan and cook the monkfish pieces on a medium heat for about 5 minutes on each side. (When turning the fish over, be very careful not to break it up.) Add the capers, anchovies, salt and pepper. Cover with a lid and cook for a further 7 minutes or until the monkfish pieces are cooked through. If you find the consistency too dry during cooking, add some of the marinade. Remove the pan from the heat with the lid still on, and leave to rest for a couple of minutes before serving.

Scrombro con pesto di bietole

Mackerel with Swiss chard pesto

People often turn their nose up at mackerel, but I love it and enjoy eating it smoked as well as fresh. This is a very simple dish to make and so very nutritious. You simply steam the fish and separately make the pesto sauce with Swiss chard. If you prefer, you can substitute spinach for the chard. Serve with some boiled new potatoes for a healthy and tasty main course!

8 SERVINGS

1 tablespoon black peppercorns

4 bay leaves

juice and zest of 1 lemon

8 fillets of fresh mackerel (weighing approx. 150g each)

FOR THE PESTO

500g Swiss chard

75g pine kernels

salt and pepper, to taste

6 tablespoons extra-virgin olive oil

TO GARNISH

a few pine kernels

a few strips of red pepper

Place about 1 litre of water in a large steamer pan together with the black peppercorns, bay leaves, lemon juice and zest.

Rinse the mackerel fillets under cold running water. Put them in the steamer basket and place it in the pan of water, prepared as above. Bring to the boil, reduce the heat and steam for 15 minutes.

In the meantime, make the pesto: first, boil the Swiss chard for about 5 minutes then drain, keeping a little of the cooking water. (Make sure you drain the leaves well; if necessary, use your hands to squeeze out any excess water.) Leave to cool. Once cool, place the Swiss chard in a blender with the pine kernels and whiz together with a little of the cooking water until you obtain a smooth consistency. Add salt and pepper to taste and the olive oil, then whiz together again until well amalgamated.

Remove the cooked fish from the steamer and serve with the Swiss chard pesto. If you prefer, heat the pesto through, otherwise it is fine served at room temperature. Garnish with a few pine kernels and strips of red pepper.

Anguilla in umido con piselli

Braised eel with peas and sage

Eel always reminds me of my younger days, when I would fish for them in the river and proudly take them home to my father, who loved to eat them. I remember he would cut the eel in pieces and roast them – they were delicious. Eel is a speciality in Italy at the Christmas Eve meal; and when I first came to England I was pleased to see that eel is popular here, too. This recipe is quick and simple and the eel marries really well with the peas.

8 SERVINGS

12 tablespoons extra-virgin olive oil

2 garlic cloves, whole

10 sage leaves

2 bay leaves

1.6kg eel, cut into chunks

salt and pepper, to taste

½ glass white wine

600g peas

600g fresh plum tomatoes, deseeded and roughly chopped

400ml vegetable stock

a handful of fresh parsley

Place an ovenproof dish on the stove and heat the olive oil. Add the garlic, sage and bay leaves and stir-fry on a medium heat until the garlic softens and turns golden. At this stage, add the eel chunks and season with salt and pepper, then cook the fish on both sides until golden. Increase the heat and add the wine, allowing it to evaporate. Stir in the peas and cook for a minute on a medium heat. Then stir in the tomatoes, half-cover with a lid and cook on a medium heat for 20 minutes, gradually adding the stock. At the end of cooking time, stir in the parsley, remove from the heat, take out the bay leaves and serve.

Branzino al profumo di arancia
Seabass with orange

Seabass is very popular in Italy and is cooked in many ways (boiled, baked or grilled), but whichever method is used it is always a delight to eat. There are even Italian songs about seabass – such is its popularity! This dish is extremely easy to prepare using very few ingredients, which will provide the subtle flavour of orange whilst preserving the delicious taste of the fish. A superb dish for a special occasion.

8 SERVINGS

2 large seabass, weighing approx. 800g each (ask your fishmonger to clean them for you)

2 garlic cloves, sliced

2 large slices of orange, peel and pith removed

salt and pepper, to taste

6 bay leaves

a handful of fresh parsley, finely chopped

extra-virgin olive oil, for drizzling

freshly squeezed juice of 3 oranges

½ glass white wine

2 oranges, peel and pith removed and thinly sliced, to garnish

a bunch of fresh bay leaves, to garnish

Preheat the oven to 180°C/350°F/gas 4.

Wash the seabass under a cold running tap and dry with kitchen towel. In the slit of the bellies, place some garlic, orange slices, salt and pepper, 2 bay leaves and some parsley.

Drizzle a large ovenproof dish with olive oil. (Use one large enough to accommodate both fish, or use 2 smaller ones.) Place the fish in the dish, or dishes. Pour over the orange juice, wine and remaining bay leaves and season with salt and pepper. Cover with foil and place in the preheated oven for about 50 minutes or until the fish are cooked through. Check them from time to time. Take off the foil, turn off the heat and leave in the oven for a couple of minutes to rest, then remove. Discard the bay leaves, garlic, orange slices and as much of the parsley as you can from the bellies of the fish.

Fillet each seabass and carefully divide amongst individual plates. Serve each fillet with slices of orange and the juices left in the pan. Garnish with more bay leaves.

Vegetali
Vegetables

In ancient times Italy did not have a great variety of green vegetables, but the successive invasions of Greeks, Arabs and others introduced so many different plants and herbs that nowadays virtually everything grows there. It was probably the ancient Greeks who brought the cultivation of vines and olives to the Italian peninsula; and it was perhaps just a bit later that the ancient Romans began to import rice, pepper and various spices from India.

The Arabs, whose colourful mosaics and domed buildings strongly influenced Italian architecture (particularly Italian churches), also introduced citrus fruits to the country, and now Italy can boast of having its own native variety of lemon – the *sfusato Amalfitano* – which grows only on the Amalfi Coast. This lemon is harvested twice a year and has a unique shape, colour and flavour, but plants need to be covered with branches and nets during the winter months to protect them from the cold. Imitations of this variety have been attempted elsewhere, but its unique qualities are hard to duplicate because it is not mass-produced: it is cultivated in exactly the same way as it has been for centuries.

At the time of the Arab invasions, houses on the Amalfi Coast were constructed on high ground for protection – from both the sea and invaders – and to provide a lookout point for any invaders arriving by sea. The houses were surrounded by gardens which were created by bringing fertile soil up from the lowlands to create the series of stepped terraces that now dominate the mountain slopes of the entire coast, making this area – the place I was born – the paradise of beauty it still is today.

Other than citrus fruits, this region has historically been rich in flavours and aromas, due to the variety of vegetables such as artichokes, aubergines and spinach that are available, as well as local aromatic herbs such

as sage, thyme, oregano and rosemary. And nowadays the assortment is even richer, so that vegetables appear in antipasto dishes, side dishes, pasta dishes and many more.

Vegetables are eaten year round, as soon as they come into season, because that is when they are at their best – with regards to taste and nutritional content – and it is only by eating these vegetables then that we get their full flavour.

In today's food shops you can find anything you want, because food can travel so quickly and easily across national borders that nowadays there are fruit and vegetables commonly available that in years past my family could only dream of eating. Commercial greenhouses are busy producing courgettes, aubergines, peppers, tomatoes, and more, all year round – not to mention summer fruits such as cherries and strawberries in winter!

The time when seasonal foods were made into preserves to enjoy later in the year seems gone forever, but it isn't really, because the flavour of tradition still has a strong appeal. I was born in a place where the hills meet the sea and a temperate climate makes everything easier to grow; there, in Amalfi, everyone's home garden is luxuriant with beautiful vegetables.

Even though housing trends have changed and most people on the Amalfi Coast now live in modern houses or apartments, many still keep a vegetable garden (an 'orto') in the countryside where they can grow organic produce which they delight in picking and taking directly from the ground to the stove. My mother used to pick everything from the garden just before mealtimes, and in the summer she made up salads with a little bit of everything she found there: tomatoes and radishes, various kinds of lettuce and wild rocket, along with aromatic herbs such as basil, celery leaves and mint. Often I used to pick them for her, which I liked doing because I could easily recognise which ones were ripe and ready to eat. I remember that she used to inspect her garden every day. At times I thought she was talking to it – like a mother to her own precious creation. And a precious thing it was indeed, because everything that grew there ended up on our dinner table.

It was fascinating to watch the pumpkins take on colour as they became larger and larger into the autumn, or the red, yellow and green peppers that created such a kaleidoscope of colours on your plate; whether fried, roasted, or just added raw to a salad with the capers that you found growing in the cracks of country walls, looking like orchids with their beautiful pink and white flowers. I still love to pick capers for preserving in salt or vinegar. The flavour of fresh fennel bulbs is also unforgettable, but you must remember not to clean them with water, just a cloth, or they will lose their wonderful, sweet freshness. Artichokes, too, are fantastic when freshly roasted or fried, especially the tender hearts. They are usually roasted outdoors because they emit smoke, but the aroma of the garlic and parsley used to fill them can travel for miles, reaching the nostrils of neighbours who never complain because the smell is so glorious.

I don't remember there being many green-grocers' when I was growing up, just local farmers who would come into town on a Sunday morning and set up crates brimming with whatever crop they happened to have harvested that week. I still love going to the greengrocers' and markets and seeing everything laid out in perfect order, with each particular colour and smell making its separate appeal for you to buy it.

In the summer season, improvised wooden tables and stands would spring up in all the main streets of Southern Italy where, for a few pennies, you could eat your fill of cool, delicious red watermelon. Indeed, the fashion nowadays for young people returning home after a very late night out dancing is to stop and sample this divine nectar, along with enormous bowls of fruit salad.

The world may change, but young people remain the same, more or less. Today they might stop to eat watermelon after the disco, but in my day, we didn't even know what a disco was – not that that stopped us, of course, from sneaking into the local gardens at night and merrily helping ourselves just the same to the bounty of Mother Nature. We never even thought of it as a crime.

Verdure miste ripiene

Stuffed mixed vegetables

The preparation involved in this simple recipe is a little lengthy, but the end result is most impressive! I have suggested two types of filling: the meat one is surprisingly light, and when combined with the vegetables it is very tasty indeed. If you have any mixture left over, you can use it to make delicious meatballs that can be lightly coated in flour and then either shallow-fried or baked in the oven. The vegetarian filling has an almost soufflé texture and a lovely cheesy flavour. If serving these stuffed vegetables as a main course, I suggest half a pepper, 1 tomato, 1 onion and half a courgette per person – you really don't need any extra accompaniments!

12 SERVINGS

3 yellow peppers

3 red peppers

12 large, ripe tomatoes (such as *ramati* or beef tomatoes)

12 medium-sized red onions

6 large courgettes

MEAT FILLING

3 tablespoons extra-virgin olive oil

1 garlic clove, finely chopped

400g minced beef

400g minced pork

3 eggs

100g Parmesan cheese, freshly grated

a handful of parsley, finely chopped

salt and pepper, to taste

300g country bread, crust removed then soaked in a little cold milk before having all the excess moisture squeezed out (use your hands to do this)

First prepare the vegetables: wash the peppers, cut off the tops (they should resemble little lids) and set aside. Remove and discard the seeds and white bits inside. Wash the tomatoes and slice off the tops, putting them to one side to use as lids, and scoop out the pulp. Peel the onions and slice into them about a quarter of the way down in order to be able to remove the cavity, which should be set aside. Wash the courgettes, cut them in half lengthways and scoop out the pulp, which, again, you should set aside.

Preheat the oven to 200°C/400°F/gas 6.

To make the meat filling for the courgettes and onions: finely chop the excess onion pieces and the courgette pulp. Heat the olive oil in a small frying pan and add the garlic, the finely chopped onion and the courgette pulp. Stir-fry on a medium heat until the vegetables have softened. Set aside.

In a large bowl, mix together the minced beef and pork, the eggs, Parmesan, parsley, salt and pepper. Add the softened bread and the onion and courgette pulp. Mix everything together until well amalgamated (this is easiest done with your hands), then stuff the onions and courgettes with the mixture.

To make the vegetarian filling for the peppers and tomatoes: in a large bowl, mix together the coarse breadcrumbs and the eggs, the Parmesan, pecorino, salt, pepper and oregano until well amalgamated. Stuff the peppers and tomatoes.

Pour the wine and stock into a large ovenproof dish or divide it between two dishes. Arrange all the filled vegetables in the dish or dishes, drizzle with the olive oil and cover with foil. Place in

VEGETARIAN FILLING

400g country bread, made into large breadcrumbs

8 eggs

100g Parmesan cheese, freshly grated

75g pecorino cheese, freshly grated

salt and pepper, to taste

a pinch of dried oregano

175ml white wine

175ml vegetable stock

extra-virgin olive oil, for drizzling

the preheated oven for 20 minutes then remove them and lower the heat to 180°C/350°F/gas 4. Place the lids on the peppers and tomatoes, replace the foil and return to the oven and bake for 25 minutes. Remove the foil and bake for a further 15 minutes. Remove from the oven and leave to rest for a couple of minutes. Serve either straight from the oven dishes or carefully transfer the vegetables to serving plates. The stuffed vegetables can be eaten hot or cold, and so can be made in advance.

Tip: Use really good-quality country bread which is a day old, as this will make a huge difference to your fillings, both texture and taste-wise.

Bastoncini fritti alle erbe

Herby chips

I don't normally cook chips, but since one of my daughters, Olivia, likes them so much I started making them at home. To give them more flavour, I coat them in mixed herbs – and they are really yummy!

8 SERVINGS

10 tablespoons mixed herbs, finely chopped (such as rosemary, sage and chives)

10 tablespoons good-quality breadcrumbs (make your own with good country bread)

1.5kg new potatoes (try to get the largest size you can)

4 egg whites, slightly beaten

oil, for frying

salt, to taste

Mix together the herbs and breadcrumbs on a plate.

Cut the potatoes into chips, rinse them in cold water and drain. Dip them in the egg whites then coat them in the herb mixture. Repeat this with both the egg whites and herb mixture. Leave to rest for a couple of minutes.

Meanwhile, heat the oil in a saucepan or a deep fryer. When hot, fry the chips until golden and drain on kitchen towel. Sprinkle with salt and enjoy!

Carciofi stufati con crostini
Braised artichokes with crostini

This is a really easy way of preparing artichokes. Basically, once you've cleaned them, you just put them and all the other ingredients into a big pot and cook. Nutritionally, artichokes are light and easily digestible, very good for you and packed with vitamins and iron.

I've used baby onions in this recipe because they are really sweet and delicious, but if you can't get them, replace them with small red onions cut into quarters – if they are quite big onions, cut them into 8 segments.

These braised artichokes are delicious served as a starter, main course or even as a side dish.

8 SERVINGS

juice of 2 lemons

8 medium-sized artichokes (including the stems)

400g baby onions

6 tablespoons white wine vinegar

300ml white wine

600ml water

6 anchovy fillets

2 tablespoons capers

2 garlic cloves

½ red chilli, finely chopped (optional)

salt, to taste

8 tablespoons extra-virgin olive oil

a handful of fresh parsley, finely chopped

FOR THE CROSTINI

8 slices of hard country bread

a drizzle of extra-virgin olive oil

a pinch of salt

a sprinkle of dried oregano

Prepare a large bowl with some cold water and lemon juice. Clean the artichokes, removing the outer leaves at the bottom and trimming the tops. Cut and peel the stems, slice them lengthways and place them in the lemon water. Cut the artichokes in half, discarding any hairs, and place them immediately in the lemon water, too, to prevent discoloration.

Drain the artichokes and their stems and place them in a large saucepan together with the onions, vinegar, wine, water, anchovy fillets, capers, garlic cloves, chilli (if using), salt and olive oil. Cover with a lid and cook over a medium heat for about 40 minutes or until the artichokes are tender, stirring from time to time and adding more water if necessary.

Towards the end of cooking time, make the crostini: drizzle the slices of bread with a little olive oil and sprinkle all over with salt and oregano. Place in an oven preheated to 200°C/400°F/gas 6 for about 10 minutes or until golden.

Remove the artichokes from the heat, sprinkle with parsley and serve with the crostini.

Zucchini e pomodori al forno

Baked courgettes and tomatoes

This is a very easy, tasty way of combining courgettes and tomatoes; they can sometimes be a little bland, so here I have livened them up with a little marjoram and Parmesan cheese. It makes a lovely side dish to accompany meat and fish. Make sure you get really fresh courgettes, otherwise they tend to taste bitter; fresh courgettes are hard and the skin is bright green in colour.

8 SERVINGS

10 tablespoons extra-virgin olive oil

6 medium-sized tomatoes, cut into 6mm round slices

6 medium-sized courgettes, cut into 6mm round slices

salt and pepper, to taste

leaves of 4 sprigs of fresh marjoram

6 tablespoons Parmesan cheese, grated

Preheat the oven to 220°C/425°F/gas 7.

Drizzle 2 tablespoons of the olive oil into a large ovenproof dish. Arrange alternate slices of tomatoes and courgettes in the dish so that they are overlapping. Season with salt and pepper, drizzle with 6 tablespoons of olive oil, sprinkle with the marjoram leaves and top with the Parmesan cheese.

Bake in the oven for 4–5 minutes or until the cheese begins to turn golden. Remove, drizzle with the remaining olive oil and serve immediately.

Verza con castagne

Savoy cabbage with chestnuts

This old, traditional recipe used to be made with more stock and eaten as a soup in times when there wasn't much choice at the market and times were hard. I had always heard stories about this soup from my grandparents, and they would threaten me with eating it when I was young and had been naughty! This wasn't because the soup was horrible in any way, but because it reminded my grandparents of those dark, grim days when food was scarce. Little did they know that some of my favourite foods are chestnuts and that I love all types of cabbage! So I have combined these ingredients to create a delicious vegetable dish that can accompany all kinds of meat, or can even be eaten on its own with lots of good bread.

8–10 SERVINGS

600g chestnuts (with shells on)

10 tablespoons extra-virgin olive oil

2 onions, finely chopped

100g pancetta, finely chopped

2kg Savoy cabbage, washed and chopped into thin strips

salt and pepper, to taste

800ml vegetable stock

With a sharp knife, make a small incision in each of the chestnuts. Bring a saucepan of slightly salted water to the boil, add the chestnuts and cook them for 7 minutes. Drain and allow them to cool a little. Peel them while they are still warm as cold chestnuts are very difficult to peel.

In a large saucepan, heat the olive oil, sweat the onions, then add the pancetta and stir-fry for a few minutes or until the pancetta turns golden. At this stage, add the cabbage strips and a pinch of salt and stir well. Reduce the heat to medium, cover with a lid and cook for 10 minutes, checking to ensure the cabbage doesn't stick or burn. Add the stock and continue to cook for a further 20 minutes with the lid half-on. Five minutes before the end of cooking time, stir in the peeled chestnuts and some black pepper. Remove from the heat, leave to rest for a couple of minutes, then serve.

Tip: Cabbage has a tendency to smell throughout cooking, so if you don't like the smell, parboil the cabbage first for about 5 minutes, drain well, then proceed as above.

Melanzane con noci e pecorino

Walnut-crusted aubergine rolls stuffed with mozzarella and Parma ham

Here's a different way of serving one of Southern Italy's best-loved vegetables – the aubergine. This recipe takes a little time to prepare, but it is very simple and well worth the effort. The aubergines are coated with a crunchy walnut crust and later filled with mozzarella, Parma ham and rocket. These rolls are delicious served hot or cold as a starter, a side dish or as nibbles at parties.

8 SERVINGS

300g breadcrumbs

150g walnuts, shelled, finely chopped

4 eggs

salt and pepper, to taste

50g pecorino Romano cheese, freshly grated

4 long aubergines, sliced ½cm lengthways (get the long, thin variety)

olive oil, for shallow frying

Parma ham slices (you need equal numbers of these and aubergine slices)

150g mozzarella cheese, cut into slices

a few basil leaves

a few rocket leaves

Mix together the breadcrumbs and the finely chopped walnuts. Beat the eggs with a little salt, then mix in the grated pecorino. Take the slices of aubergine and coat both sides in the beaten egg, then in the breadcrumb and walnut mixture. Make sure you press the coating onto the aubergine well. I suggest you do this with your hands, otherwise when you are frying them all the bits will come away.

Heat the oil in a large frying pan and, when hot, lower in the coated aubergine slices, just a few at a time, and fry them on both sides. When golden, remove and drain on kitchen towel.

Place a slice of Parma ham, mozzarella and a couple of basil leaves on each slice of aubergine and roll it up, securing it with toothpicks, if necessary. Do this quickly while the aubergine slices are still warm, otherwise they are likely to crack as they are being rolled.

Place the finished rolls on a large serving dish and garnish with rocket leaves or baby salad leaves.

Zucca all'agro dolce

Sweet and sour pumpkin

This is a very simple side dish that is quick and easy to prepare, and which goes perfectly with game and poultry dishes.

8–10 SERVINGS

2kg pumpkin (total weight, with skin)

16 tablespoons extra-virgin olive oil

6 garlic cloves, roughly chopped

50g capers

salt and pepper (just a pinch of salt – you can be generous with the pepper)

10 tablespoons white wine vinegar

100g sugar

a handful of fresh mint leaves, finely chopped

Peel and deseed the pumpkin and roughly chop it into 1cm cubes.

In a large frying pan, heat the olive oil and sauté the pumpkin cubes until they start to change colour. Add the garlic and capers and season with salt and pepper.

In a dish, mix together the vinegar and sugar until the sugar dissolves. Add this mixture to the pumpkin, stir well and continue to cook for about 10 minutes or until soft. Serve immediately with some freshly chopped mint.

Broccoli con peperoncino e olive

Broccoli with chilli and olives

This is a really simple dish that is popular in all regions of Southern Italy. It is usually made with the long-stemmed flat broccoli which is known in Britain as turnip tops, and which can sometimes be found in certain supermarkets and markets. However, for this recipe I have used the normal everyday broccoli that accompanies many British Sunday lunches and everyday meals. So next time you cook broccoli, why not spice it up a bit? You can substitute cauliflower for the broccoli, if you prefer. Whichever vegetable you use, you can add this to freshly cooked pasta for a quick, nutritious and delicious meal! *Buon appetito!*

10–12 SERVINGS

2kg broccoli florets

salt

10 tablespoons extra-virgin olive oil

3 garlic cloves, left whole

1 small red chilli, finely chopped

8 anchovy fillets

4 tablespoons green olives, pitted and halved

Bring a large saucepan of slightly salted water to the boil, then drop in the broccoli and cook for 4 minutes.

Meanwhile, heat the olive oil in a large frying pan, add the garlic, chilli and anchovies and stir-fry for a couple of minutes. Stir in the olives. Drain the broccoli and add to the frying pan. Stir-fry everything quickly, then reduce the heat, cover with a lid and cook for 3 minutes. Check the broccoli is tender, if it is not, add a couple of tablespoons of hot water and continue to cook until it is done. Remove the lid, increase the heat and cook for a further 2 minutes. Serve immediately.

Parmigiana alla melanzane in pomodoro fresco

Aubergine 'parmigiana' with fresh tomato

I love aubergine *parmigiana*, and so do most Italians – especially in the South. The traditional way of making this dish is in layers in an ovenproof dish, and it is the most simple and satisfying comfort food that always reminds me of home. This is another, more up-to-date version, which is just as easy to prepare and looks impressive when served. In this recipe the layers of fried aubergine, tomato sauce, basil and cheese go inside the cavity of a scooped-out beef tomato, which gives the *parmigiana* a nice flavour.

I have used scamorza here, which is a smoked mozzarella cheese that can be found in good delis, but if you can't get it the hard mozzarella, Parmesan or even Cheddar will suffice. If you prefer, you can use courgettes instead of aubergines and follow exactly the same method outlined below. This *parmigiana* is ideal as a starter – serve one tomato per person – or as a side dish, or you can serve more for a main course. You can prepare these in advance and cook them in the oven just before they are needed.

12 SERVINGS

12 beef tomatoes, ripe but firm (try to get large ones that are all roughly the same size)

8 tablespoons extra-virgin olive oil

2 small onions, finely chopped

salt and pepper, to taste

a handful of basil leaves

800g aubergine

plain flour, to coat

3 eggs, beaten with a little salt

oil, for frying

200g smoked mozzarella

Using a sharp knife, slice the tops off the tomatoes to make lids. With a small spoon or scoop, remove the pulp inside the tomatoes and reserve.

Heat the olive oil in a pan, sweat the onions, then add the tomato pulp, salt and pepper and half of the basil leaves. Stir well, reduce the heat to medium and cook with the lid half-on for about 20 minutes, checking and stirring from time to time.

Meanwhile, put a little salt inside the cavity of each tomato and turn each one upside down to allow any remaining moisture to escape.

Slice the aubergine into thin rounds, coat them in plain flour (shaking off any excess), then dip them in the beaten egg. Heat the frying oil in a large pan and, when hot, drop in the aubergine slices and fry until golden. Drain on kitchen towel and sprinkle a little salt all over.

Preheat the oven to 200°C/400°F/gas 6.

At this stage you are ready to assemble your ingredients in the cavity of each tomato. Begin with a slice of aubergine, then top with some tomato sauce, followed by a basil leaf and then a slice

of mozzarella. Repeat the layers until you end up with a slice of aubergine at the top. Do this with all the tomatoes in turn and, when finished, top with the tomato lid.

Place the filled tomatoes in an ovenproof dish, sprinkle with salt and pepper and drizzle with some olive oil. Place in the preheated oven and bake for about 25 minutes or until the tomatoes have become soft. Remove and place on a large serving dish or individual plates and garnish with some basil. Serve hot or warm.

Insalata tiepida di radicchio, zucca e cipolla rossa

Warm salad of radicchio, pumpkin and sweet red onions

This lovely warm salad is perfect during the winter months when the radicchio di Treviso and pumpkins are in season. It is very simple to make, but you need to work quickly at the end so that it can be served warm. This salad is delicious as a starter or as an accompaniment to a main course – place it in the middle of the table so that everyone can tuck in.

8 SERVINGS

100g raisins

2 tablespoons white wine

2 medium-sized, sweet red onions, sliced into segments

600g pumpkin, clean weight, finely sliced

leaves of 2 sprigs of thyme

1 tablespoon extra-virgin olive oil

2 radicchio rosso of Treviso, cut in half lengthways (or use ordinary radicchio)

2 tablespoons pine kernels, lightly toasted

FOR THE DRESSING

8 tablespoons extra-virgin olive oil

5 tablespoons balsamic vinegar

salt and pepper, to taste

Place the raisins in a glass with the wine and leave to soften.

Heat a griddle pan on the stove and roast the onions and sliced pumpkin for about 4 minutes on each side, sprinkling with the leaves of 1 of the thyme sprigs.

In the meantime, lightly grease a large frying pan with the olive oil and heat. When hot, add the radicchio and sauté it for 2 minutes on either side, making sure it does not burn but heats through.

In a small bowl, mix together the ingredients for the dressing until well amalgamated. Drain the raisins well and squeeze the excess moisture out using your hands, then put in another bowl. Set both bowls aside.

Place the slices of warm, softened onion, pumpkin and radicchio on a large serving dish, scatter with the pine kernels and raisins and pour over the dressing. Sprinkle with the remaining thyme leaves and serve immediately.

Finocchi al forno con pomodoro marinato e patate

Baked fennel with marinated tomatoes and potatoes

It is said that fennel is good for you and has many healing properties, such as aiding digestion; aside from that, it is delicious, both when eaten raw in salads or when cooked. This recipe is simple to prepare and can be served as a vegetarian main course or as a side dish to accompany fish. If you don't like the strong taste of fennel seeds, you can either use less of them or omit them altogether.

600g tinned cherry tomatoes

2 garlic cloves, finely chopped

1 teaspoon fennel seeds, lightly ground

2 teaspoons dried oregano

salt and pepper, to taste

200ml vegetable stock

1kg potatoes, peeled and cut into slices 1cm thick

8 medium-sized fennel (cleaned and sliced widthways)

8 tablespoons extra-virgin olive oil, plus extra for greasing

a handful of parsley, finely chopped

Preheat the oven to 200°C/400°F/gas 6.

In a bowl, mix together the tomatoes, garlic, fennel seeds, oregano and a little salt. Mix in the stock and leave to marinate.

Grease an ovenproof dish with a little olive oil and line with half of the potato slices. Then top with all the fennel segments, followed by the tomato mixture. Lastly, top with the remaining potato slices. Drizzle with the olive oil. Cover with aluminium foil and place in the oven for 30 minutes. Remove the foil, increase the heat to 220°C/425°F/gas 7 and continue to bake for a further 15 minutes.

Remove from the oven, sprinkle with freshly ground black pepper and finely chopped parsley and serve.

Verdure di primavera al cartoccio
Spring vegetables baked in foil

Spring is when fresh vegetables are back in season. The fresher they are, and the more in season they are, the better they taste. This is a wonderfully quick and simple recipe. By baking the vegetables in foil, all the flavour is retained so when you open the parcel, you get a lovely aroma, sure to impress your guests! They are ideal with fish or meat, or just put them in the centre of the table and eat them with lots of good bread. You can of course replace the vegetables here with whatever you find at the market or whatever is in season. If you are cooking for smaller numbers of people, you can just make one larger parcel if you prefer, but for large numbers, individual ones are much easier to handle!

8 SERVINGS

8 asparagus spears, with any hard pieces of stem trimmed off

2 large chicory bulbs, sliced lengthways into quarters

2 radicchio heads, quartered

4 small courgettes, sliced into thickish batons

1 yellow pepper, sliced into thickish strips lengthways

1 red pepper, sliced into thickish strips lengthways

handful of fresh basil leaves

salt and pepper

12 tablespoons extra-virgin olive oil

6 tablespoons lemon juice

aluminium foil

Preheat the oven to 200°C/400°F/gas 6.

Clean the vegetables carefully and dry them well on kitchen towel.

Lay out 8 sheets of aluminium foil large enough to accommodate a serving each of mixed vegetables. In each piece of foil, place 1 asparagus, 1 piece of chicory, 1 piece of radicchio, a couple of slices of courgettes, a few strips of yellow and red pepper, a few basil leaves and sprinkle with salt and pepper. Close the sheets of foil tightly. Place them carefully on a baking tray and cook in the preheated oven for 20–25 minutes.

Meanwhile, in a small bowl, whisk together the olive oil and lemon juice.

When the pockets are ready, remove from the oven, open them up and drizzle the dressing over the vegetables. Serve right away, because they are best served hot.

Salsina per verdure

Dressing for vegetables

This dressing is ideal for pouring over raw or cooked vegetables. For example, this could be used as an alternative dressing for the *Spring Vegetables Baked in Foil* (see page 148), or to dress grilled or barbecued vegetables, or as a marinade for raw vegetables.

MAKES ENOUGH FOR 1.5KG OF FRESH VEGETABLES

150ml extra-virgin olive oil

5 tablespoons balsamic vinegar

2 garlic cloves, finely chopped

1 red chilli, finely chopped (optional)

2 tablespoons of parsley, finely chopped

2 tablespoons of a mixture of thyme, chives and basil, finely chopped

5 peppercorns

salt, to taste

In a small bowl, combine all the ingredients and beat with a small whisk or fork until well amalgamated.

Feste e Scampagnate
Picnics, Parties and Days Out

Italians don't really need an excuse to celebrate: each time they sit at the table, it is a feast! However, on important occasions, a party is organised. This can be at Christmas time, certainly New Year's Eve and saint's days, such as the patron saints of a particular town.

In my village on the Amalfi Coast, we still celebrate the feast of our patron saint, Santa Trofimena, when all the villagers get together for a big party. The statue of Santa Trofimena is paraded through the village followed by a procession of people. Fireworks are let off by the sea, filling the night sky with bright lights; and rows of tables are set out on the streets filled with all sorts of delicious food and treats. I was brought up with this tradition and even today, when I have time, I enjoy going back to Minori for this celebration. And I'm not alone; lots of friends who have emigrated to other countries also return for this. I think with the busy lives that we all lead and the different paths life has taken us on, at least for this one day in the year, we are all bound together and transported back to our roots. On that day we can forget the pressures and worries of life in the sound knowledge that we are gathered together in harmony and peace to pay homage to the mother of all the citizens of Minori.

Then there are parties held at home for birthdays, anniversaries, christenings and holy communion celebrations, even though the latter two are now more usually held at local or country restaurants. However, when I was young, these were traditionally done at home and even if there were lots of people, you all squeezed in and somehow room was made for everyone. Of course, food was plentiful. I remember on these occasions, we had so much food left over that my mother would make food parcels to give to our guests on their way out! I loved a full house and when everyone had gone, I would go into the kitchen to see what was left over for us

and I knew this would be for our lunch the next day.

I have always enjoyed days out, especially in the countryside or by the sea. As a child, I was extremely lucky to have both sea and mountains on my doorstep, so I had the choice of where to spend my time. It was fun to organise picnics once spring had arrived. The traditional day for this to begin, and still is today, is Easter Monday, *Pasquetta*, when most Italian families prepare a picnic basket and head off to green areas to enjoy eating outdoors. Our *Pasquetta* was an amazing event, with people bringing pots and pans, camping gas stoves, barbecues and even erecting tents and folding beds so they could stay overnight and really enjoy living outdoors! The aroma wafting from the various pots was wonderful as we would head towards the designated picnic spot to join the other villagers and enjoy a lovely day out amongst friends and family, eating, drinking, discussing life, playing cards while the children ran around playing hide and seek.

Then there were quieter days out, such as barbecues on the beach with a few friends, something that is now forbidden on our beaches and eating outside on warm summer evenings, especially when my father lit the barbecue and we would enjoy home-made sausages, the new season's artichokes or freshly caught fish lightly cooked and drizzled with olive oil and lemon juice. Nowadays, I enjoy cooking in my outdoor kitchen at home, where I have a barbecue, wood-burning stove and my beloved wood-burning oven. When we have parties or groups of people round, I often make pizza or roast some meat and vegetables in the oven – such simple dishes to make, but the taste is sublime! When making pizza, I usually get each guest, especially the children – they love it – to make their own, under my instruction of course! It makes for a fun day and when they leave, they are usually armed with a loaf or two of bread as well. Each time I light the oven, I have to make bread; it comes out so natural, so pure, that you don't want to eat the bought stuff any more.

But my favourite outing was during the autumn when it was mushroom season. I loved going up to the mountains with my mother to collect the edible ones: some were for her remedies and the rest we would take home to eat. Or sometimes, as a treat, she took the camping gas, a small frying pan, garlic, chilli, olive oil and parsley and we would cook some up and eat them with a little bread. I still do this today with my family and friends. I supply each person in the party with a basket and small knife and after we have all collected a sufficient amount, I switch on the camping gas and either sauté the mushrooms like my mother used to or make a mixed mushroom risotto. A real treat after a long, tiring morning looking for mushrooms and so nice to think that after much walking and collecting, you are now eating the food you picked with your own hands!

Verdure in crosta di parmigiano
Parmesan-crusted vegetables

These moreish, light and fluffy fritters are a delight. I have only coated vegetables and herbs, but you could use the same batter for bits of leftover cooked meat or fish and any other vegetable or fruit you like – you can be very creative with this recipe! These fritters make a lovely starter or they can also be served with drinks or at parties. They are fun to make for children's parties, too, and it might even encourage the little ones to eat vegetables!

12 SERVINGS

12 cauliflower florets

12 broccoli florets

2 medium-sized courgettes, cut into thin chips

1 large parsnip, cut into thin chips

2 fennel, cut into small segments

24 sun-dried tomato halves (not the ones in olive oil)

12 courgette flowers (if in season)

24 sage leaves

24 basil leaves

12 radicchio leaves

FOR THE BATTER

20g fresh yeast

300ml lukewarm sparkling mineral water

300g oo flour or plain flour

pinch of salt

100g Parmesan cheese, freshly grated

200ml milk

oil, for frying

First make the batter: dissolve the yeast in the lukewarm water. In a large bowl, sift the flour and salt, make a well in the centre and add the yeast mixture. Add the Parmesan and milk. Mix well and beat with a whisk until you obtain a smooth batter. Cover with a cloth and leave to rise in a warm place for an hour or until it has almost doubled in size.

Meanwhile, prepare all the vegetables, washing and cutting them as outlined in the ingredients list. Drain and place them on kitchen towel to dry.

Pour an abundant amount of oil into a large pan or deep fryer, and while it is heating begin dipping the vegetables into the batter, coating them well. When the oil is hot, drop the battered vegetables in a few at a time and fry them for a couple of minutes until puffy and golden. Lift them out using a slotted spoon and drain them on pieces of kitchen towel. Serve immediately.

Tip: Should the oil become brown in colour, change it; otherwise your fritters will also turn a horrible brown colour.

Pasta al forno
Baked pasta

Pasta al forno is one of the most popular party dishes in Italy. This is my version of it which is typical of where I come from, but you can mix the pasta with other ingredients: such as a plain tomato sauce, a tomato sauce with vegetables, or a cheese sauce. It is really simple to make for lots of people and can be made in advance and put in the oven just before serving. For this recipe, I have used the famous Italian meat ragù, which gives the tomato sauce a lovely rich meaty flavour. You don't leave the cooked meat in the dish, but keep it for a family meal the next day.

A baked pasta dish is a welcome addition to the buffet table and, in my experience, is always finished quickly!

To make the ragù: heat the olive oil in a large saucepan, then add the onion and sweat it. Add the spare ribs and beef chunks, the bay leaf, some salt and pepper and seal the meat well on all sides. Add the wine with the diluted tomato concentrate and allow it to evaporate. Mix in the tomatoes and basil leaves. Bring to the boil, then reduce the heat and cover with a lid (leaving it slightly open) and gently simmer for 2½ hours, stirring from time to time. Check for seasoning and, if necessary, add more salt and pepper.

Once the sauce is ready, remove the pieces of meat and the bay leaf.

Cook the pasta until al dente, drain and return to the saucepan. Add 3 ladlefuls of the ragù and half of the grated Parmesan. Mix together well. Add the cubed mozzarella, ricotta, salami, 50g of the Parmesan and most of the ragù (reserving a couple of ladlefuls). Mix together well, but gently, so as not to break the pasta.

Preheat the oven to 180°C/350°F/gas 4.

Line the ovenproof dish with one ladleful of tomato sauce, then spoon over the mixed pasta. Add the egg quarters, pushing them down into the pasta. Cover with the remaining tomato sauce and sprinkle with the remaining Parmesan. Place in the oven for 1 hour. Remove, leave to rest for 5 minutes, then serve.

12 SERVINGS

FOR THE RAGÙ SAUCE

8 tablespoons extra-virgin olive oil

1 small onion, finely chopped

6 pork spare ribs, cut in half

500g beef skirting, cut into large chunks

1 bay leaf

salt and pepper, to taste

150ml red wine

3 tablespoons tomato concentrate (diluted in the wine)

5 x 400g tins of plum tomatoes, finely chopped

a handful of fresh basil leaves, torn

1kg rigatoni pasta

200g Parmesan cheese, freshly grated

400g hard mozzarella, cubed

300g ricotta

200g salami, sliced and chopped

6 eggs, hard-boiled, peeled and cut into quarters

Bocconcini di polenta con baccalá e rucola
Grilled polenta bites with salt cod and rocket

These bites make a lovely party dish or starter for a formal dinner. Salt cod is easily available in this country; try your fishmonger or good Italian deli. If you prefer, you could use fresh cod, but I think salt cod combines with polenta really well. I have made these bites as circles 8cm in diameter, but you could make them smaller or use a different shaped pastry cutter or, for a more rustic look, cut them in roughly squared shapes with a sharp knife.

MAKES 14 BITES

500g salt cod

2 bay leaves

2 celery stalks

1 lemon, cut in half

1.5 litre water

salt, to taste

350g polenta

2 garlic cloves, squashed and left whole

10 tablespoons extra-virgin olive oil, plus extra for greasing

a bunch of rocket

12 cherry tomatoes, quartered

300g provolone cheese, cut into small cubes

1 round pastry cutter, 8cm in diameter

First, place the salt cod in a container, cover with cold water and leave to soak for 48 hours. Change the water every 12 hours. (This is done to remove the salt.) Take it out of the water and cut it into chunks. Place the cod in a saucepan and cover it with clean cold water together with the bay leaves, celery and lemon halves. Cover with a lid, place on the heat and boil for 2 minutes. Remove the fish and drain, discarding the other ingredients. Allow to cool for a couple of minutes, then remove the skin and any bones you find. Set aside.

To make the polenta: put the water and a pinch of salt into a non-stick saucepan and bring to the boil. Gradually add the polenta, stirring all the time until it has been amalgamated, then reduce the heat. (This is important as polenta does tend to bubble quite a bit.) Beware of any lumps forming; if they do, just beat very energetically until the lumps have dissolved. Cook the polenta according to the instructions on the packet. If you are using the traditional variety, it usually takes about 40 minutes to cook, stirring all the time. The quick variety should only take about 5 minutes.

As soon as the polenta is cooked, pour it into a lightly oiled, large, fairly flat dish and leave to cool. Once cool, cut out the circles or other shapes with your pastry cutter or knife. Place on a slightly oiled baking tray, drizzle with a little olive oil and place under a hot grill for 7 minutes or until golden. Turn them over and grill for another 7 minutes.

Meanwhile, place the cod in a bowl together with the garlic and olive oil. Mix well. In another bowl, mix together the rocket, cherry tomatoes and a little salt – but be careful when adding this as the fish can still be quite salty, even after rinsing. Then,

very gently, so as not to break the fish, add the rocket and cherry tomatoes to the cod.

Top each of the polenta bites with some cheese and return them to the hot grill for a couple of minutes or until the cheese has softened. Top with the cod mixture, place on a large serving dish and serve.

Arrosto di maiale con senape, mela e speck

Roast pork with mustard, apple and speck

As it is extremely easy to prepare, this is the perfect dish for when you are having lots of people over for Sunday lunch, or for a party. It is delicious eaten hot or cold.

12 SERVINGS

2kg jacket of pork, deboned

80g butter, softened

40g mustard seeds

salt and pepper, to taste

2 apples, washed, cored and cut into slices

80g speck, thinly sliced

4 sprigs of thyme, cut into pieces

2 sprigs of rosemary, cut into pieces

extra-virgin olive oil, for drizzling

6 tablespoons white wine

400ml stock, kept hot

kitchen string or raffia, for tying the pork

Preheat the oven to 200°C/400°F/gas 6.

Unroll the jacket of pork and set aside.

In a small bowl, mix together the butter, mustard seeds and salt and pepper. Spread half of this mixture inside the pork, and on top of this arrange the pieces of apple, half of the speck and all of the thyme and rosemary, reserving a few sprigs for the outside. Very carefully, roll up the pork jacket and tie tightly with kitchen string or raffia and ensure the filling does not escape.

Spread the remaining butter mixture all over the outside of the pork and place the remaining sprigs of thyme and rosemary under the pieces of string, so that they stay in place during cooking. Top with the remaining slices of speck and drizzle with some olive oil. Reduce the oven to 180°C/350°F/gas 4, place the pork in a roasting tin and cook it in the oven for 20 minutes. Remove, pour over the wine, put back in the oven for 5 minutes. Remove again and pour over a couple of ladlefuls of the stock.

Return to the oven and continue to roast for approximately 2 hours or until the pork is cooked through. During cooking, baste the pork from time to time and gradually add stock, as required.

When cooked, remove the pork from the oven and let it rest for 10 minutes before slicing and serving with the gravy juices.

Bruschetta con prosciutto crudo e fichi caramellati

Bruschetta with Parma ham and caramelised figs

Making bruschetta is an excellent way of using up leftover country bread and it is delicious with all sorts of toppings. Here I have given you three recipe ideas that go together really well. I have not given specific quantities of ingredients, as I leave this up to you – depending on the size of the bread slices you use and how many people you are feeding. You can serve bruschetta as a starter, at parties or simply as a lovely snack!

sugar (you need 1 teaspoon per fig)

fresh or dried figs

slices of good-quality country bread (approx. 1cm thick)

rocket

slices of Parma ham

If you are using dried figs, reconstitute them in some lukewarm water for about 10 minutes.

In a small pan, dissolve the sugar in a little water. Add the figs and caramelise them for a couple of minutes. Remove from the heat and set aside.

Grill the slices of bread on both sides. Remove from the heat and top with some rocket leaves, a slice of Parma ham and a couple of caramelised figs. Place on a plate and serve.

Bruschetta con pomodorini e mozzarella

Bruschetta with cherry tomatoes and mozzarella

slices of good-quality country bread (1cm thick)

cherry tomatoes

slices of mozzarella (well drained)

dried oregano

extra-virgin olive oil

salt and pepper, to taste

Preheat the oven to 200°C/400°F/gas 6.

Place the cherry tomatoes on a baking tray lined with greaseproof paper and bake in the oven for about 20 minutes or until they have softened slightly, but are not mushy.

Top the slices of bread with the mozzarella and softened tomatoes and sprinkle with oregano and salt and pepper and drizzle with some olive oil. Place them in the oven for about 10 minutes or until the bread is crusty and the mozzarella has melted. Remove, place on a plate and serve.

Bruschetta con Gorgonzola, noci e miele

Bruschetta with Gorgonzola cheese, walnuts and honey

slices of good-quality
country bread (approx.
1cm thick)
Belgian endive
Gorgonzola cheese, sliced
walnuts, roughly chopped
runny honey

Grill the slices of bread on both sides. Remove them from the
heat and top with some Belgian endive and slices of Gorgonzola
cheese. Sprinkle with some walnuts and drizzle over a little
honey to finish.

Salsina calda di aglio e acciughe
Hot garlic and anchovy dip

Also known as *Bagna cauda*, this is a delicious dipping sauce that is popular in the Piemonte region in Northern Italy and is usually served with pieces of raw vegetables. The sauce is traditionally cooked and served in terracotta pots and kept warm over a gentle flame while it is being eaten. It makes a lovely, informal starter or a perfect party piece!

12 SERVINGS

a selection of fresh vegetables for dipping (such as carrots, celery, fennel, red and yellow peppers, spring onions, cucumber, radishes)

240g butter

10 garlic cloves, finely chopped

280g anchovy fillets

400ml extra-virgin olive oil

First, prepare the vegetables. Wash and slice them into appropriate pieces for dipping and arrange them on a large serving dish.

Ideally the dip should be prepared in a terracotta pan, but use whatever you have. Heat the butter on a very low heat and add the garlic. Leave to simmer until the garlic softens, making sure it doesn't burn. Add the anchovies and stir them until they dissolve. Add the olive oil and heat through, stirring all the time.

Pour the dip into the appropriate bowl. (A terracotta bowl set over a gentle flame is best, but if you don't have one, use a fondue bowl.) Serve with the pieces of raw vegetables.

Fonduta di ciocolato bianco al limoncello

White chocolate fondue with lemon liqueur

Whilst writing this book, I found it really difficult to decide which chocolate fondue to include – white or dark – so I have put them both in. They are equally delicious and a real treat for young and old! You can make both types, as they are a delicious treat served alongside one another as an after-dinner dessert or at parties.

6 SERVINGS

fresh fruit, to serve (such as strawberries, blackberries, blueberries, kiwi slices, peaches, apricots, apple slices, grapes)

cubes of sponge or sweet breadsticks (see page 172)

160ml double cream

200ml limoncello liqueur

zest of 2 lemons

500g white chocolate, roughly chopped

Wash the fruit, cut as appropriate and arrange on a serving plate together with the sweet breadsticks or sponge cubes, or whatever you wish.

Put the cream, limoncello and lemon zest into a bowl and place it over a gentle bain-marie, stirring all the time. Add the chocolate pieces and continue to stir until it has melted and is smooth. Set the fondue container over a flame and serve with the fruit and sweet breadsticks or sponge cubes.

Tip: As white chocolate tends to become quite watery when melted (compared to dark chocolate), switch off the heat for a minute or so and it will thicken.

Fonduta di ciocolato

Dark chocolate fondue

Serve this alongside the *White Chocolate Fondue with Lemon Liqueur* (see page 168) with the same pieces of fruit and sweet breadsticks. Although equally delicious, this fondue is richer than the white chocolate one – so go easy on it!

6–8 SERVINGS

fresh fruit, to serve
(such as strawberries,
blueberries, blackberries,
kiwi slices, peaches,
apricots)

sweet breadsticks
(see page 172)

230ml water

150g sugar

250g good-quality
chocolate, roughly
chopped

60g butter, softened at
room temperature

3 tablespoons Frangelico
(Italian hazelnut liqueur)
or dark rum

Place the water and sugar in a small saucepan. Cook over a low heat until the sugar has dissolved and you obtain a syrup-like consistency. Remove and set aside.

Melt the chocolate over a bain-marie. Remove from the heat, stir in the butter until well amalgamated, then add the syrup and liqueur or rum, stirring well. Pour into a fondue bowl and set over a flame. Serve with the fruit and sweet breadsticks.

Grissini dolci
Sweet breadsticks

Grissini are usually always made to be savoury, but when I made the chocolate fondues I decided that they needed a biscuit to be dipped into them, hence I came up with these sweet grissini. The method is the same as the basic grissini recipe in my first book, *Passione*, with the simple addition of sugar and Amaretto liqueur.

These sweet breadsticks are a treat served with the fondues and, made in varying lengths, look lovely. The whole effect of these home-made breadsticks, a platter of mixed fruit and the bubbling pots of the fondues are a feast for your guests' eyes.

MAKES 12 GRISSINI

300g 00 flour or
plain flour

200g durum wheat
semolina

a pinch of salt

50g sugar

15g yeast

320ml lukewarm water

4 tablespoons Amaretto
liqueur

In a large bowl or clean work surface, mix together the flour, semolina, salt and sugar. Dissolve the yeast in the lukewarm water and add this to the flours together with the Amaretto liqueur. Mix well together until you obtain a dough-like consistency. Knead for about 10 minutes, form into a ball shape and leave to rise in a warm place, covered with a cloth, until it has doubled in size.

On a lightly floured work surface, gently roll out the dough into a square shape about the same thickness as your little finger. Using a sharp knife, cut strips approximately 1cm wide – don't worry about the length, they can be of varying sizes.

Sprinkle some semolina onto a flat baking tray. Place the grissini on the tray about 2cm apart, gently pulling them out a little at either end as you do so. (If you want the grissini to have a rounded shape, roll each strip gently with your fingers before placing it on the baking tray.) Leave in a warm place for 30 minutes or until they have doubled in size.

Preheat the oven to 240°C/475°F/gas 9.

Place the grissini in the oven for 10 minutes. Remove and reduce the oven temperature to 110°C/225°F/gas 1/4. When the oven has cooled down to this temperature, place the grissini back in for 35 minutes or until golden brown. Remove from the oven and leave to cool before serving.

Frittata di pasta

Pasta omelette

This has typically always been something that we used to take out on picnics, and still do. It is the perfect energy-giver if you have been walking a lot, as the pasta provides carbohydrate and the eggs protein. I have given you a basic recipe, but you can also make it with some tomato sauce or ham, or you could use leftover pasta. I usually use 1 egg for 2 people; you just beat the egg with the cooked pasta, then cook as below – just as you would a normal omelette. Enjoy!

12 SERVINGS

1kg spaghetti

7 eggs

salt and pepper, to taste

180g Parmesan cheese, freshly grated

60g butter, softened

1 tablespoon parsley (optional)

4 tablespoons extra-virgin olive oil

Cook the spaghetti until al dente. Drain and set aside.

In a large bowl, beat the eggs together with some salt and pepper, Parmesan, butter and parsley (if using). Add the drained spaghetti and mix well.

Place a large, non-stick pan on the heat with the olive oil. Pour in the omelette mixture, mix it with a fork or shake the pan a little, just as you would when making an omelette. Reduce the heat and allow to cook until a golden-brown crust is formed at the bottom. Flip the omelette over very carefully and continue to cook until the other side turns golden brown. Remove and serve hot or cold.

Insalata di riso

Rice salad

This is perfect for most occasions – picnics, barbecues, parties or a light lunch. It can be made the day before, as the longer it rests the better the flavour. Pack in well-sealed containers if taking on picnics or serve in a large bowl when entertaining at home.

12 SERVINGS

800g long grain rice

salt and pepper, to taste

200g green beans, topped, tailed and cut in half

300g hard mozzarella, cut into small cubes

100g green olives, pitted

1 celery stalk, finely chopped

1 carrot, finely chopped

6 cornichons, finely chopped

½ yellow pepper, sliced into small cubes

½ red pepper, sliced into small cubes

12 tablespoons extra-virgin olive oil

200g tinned tuna, drained

200g cherry tomatoes, quartered

handful of basil leaves, torn

Cook the rice with a little salt until al dente and not overcooked or mushy. Drain and rinse under cold running water, then drain well again. Set aside.

Cook the green beans until they are tender. Drain and leave to cool. Set aside.

In a large serving bowl, mix together the mozzarella, olives, green beans, celery, carrot, cornichons, yellow and red pepper, olive oil and salt and pepper. Add the rice and mix well, then add the tuna, cherry tomatoes and basil leaves. Gently mix together. Taste for seasoning and add more salt and pepper, if necessary. Leave in the fridge until ready to use.

Anguria al vino rosso e agrumi

Watermelon in red wine and citrus fruits

A perfect way to enjoy watermelon on a warm summer's day or, even better, together with a glass of chilled red wine. To serve at home, place in a punch bowl and offer some to your guests upon arrival. Not only will it refresh them, but the chilled alcohol will soon make them feel welcome!

8 SERVINGS

1 orange, washed and thinly sliced

1 lemon, washed and thinly sliced

100g sugar

30ml brandy

500ml red wine

4 mint leaves, finely chopped

rind of 1 orange, thinly sliced in strips

juice of 1 orange, strained through a sieve

1.5kg watermelon

12 mint leaves, left whole

First, prepare the wine sauce. Place the slices of orange and lemon in a bowl and add the sugar, followed by the brandy and wine. Add the chopped mint leaves and place in the fridge for 12 hours or overnight.

Remove the wine sauce from the fridge and strain through a fine sieve. Stir in the strips of orange rind and the orange juice.

Cut the watermelon into slices, discarding the black pips, then cut each slice into small, 1cm cubes. Place in a bowl together with the wine sauce and garnish with the whole mint leaves. Serve immediately.

If you are not serving this immediately or are taking it on a picnic with you, prepare it this way:

Place the strained wine and the orange juice and rind in the freezer for 10 minutes, then pour it into a thermos flask. Freezer the watermelon cubes in the same way, then place them in another thermos flask.

The flasks will keep both the wine and watermelon cool until required, which is ideal if you are going on a summer picnic, but remember to take a bowl or empty container with you so you can mix the watermelon and wine together before serving. Don't forget the fresh mint leaves, too!

Torta salata con scarola e scamorza
Savoury escarole and smoked mozzarella pie

This pie was always a must when we went on picnics or long journeys. The filling usually consisted of leftovers (and what these were varied, depending on the season), but the pie casing was always made from leftover bread dough. It is an ideal dish to take with you when you are out and about as it is like a ready-made sandwich – but a million times tastier. This type of savoury pie is tasty eaten cold, so it's perfect for both picnics and parties!

12 SERVINGS

½ quantity of basic bread dough (see page 194)

5 tablespoons extra-virgin olive oil

1 teaspoon freshly ground black pepper

FOR THE FILLING

1.5kg escarole, washed and sliced into small strips

10 tablespoons extra-virgin olive oil

2 garlic cloves

50g capers

100g black olives, pitted

50g pine kernels

40g raisins

8 anchovy fillets

150g smoked mozzarella, cut into cubes

salt and pepper, to taste

1 round cake tin, 26cm in diameter

cocktail stick or fork, for pricking dough

Make the bread dough. After the first rising, place the dough on a lightly floured, clean work surface and add to it 5 tablespoons of olive oil and half a teaspoon of black pepper. Knead together well for about 5 minutes, then form the dough into a ball, cover it with a cloth and put it in a warm place for 30 minutes to rise again.

Meanwhile, make the filling: bring a large saucepan of slightly salted water to the boil, then add the escarole strips and cook for 5 minutes. Remove using a slotted spoon and drain well, eliminating all the excess water. Set aside.

In a frying pan, heat 6 tablespoons of the olive oil and add the garlic cloves, allowing them to infuse for a few minutes. Add the escarole and stir-fry for 5 minutes, then remove the garlic. Add the capers, olives, pine kernels and raisins. Cook on a medium heat for 10 minutes. Remove from the heat and add the anchovy fillets and smoked mozzarella. Taste the mixture before adding salt and pepper, if needed.

Preheat the oven to 240°C/465°F/gas 9.

Next, assemble the pie. Take the bread dough and divide into two pieces, one slightly larger than the other. Take the larger piece and roll it out to a roughly round shape, 4mm thick, on a lightly floured, clean work surface. Line the cake tin with this piece and make holes all over the dough with a cocktail stick or a fork. Spoon in the filling and drizzle the remaining olive oil over it. Roll the other piece of dough to the same thickness (4mm) and use it to cover the filling. Make holes all over the dough top, as before.

Reduce the oven to 220°C/425°F/gas 7 and cook the pie in the oven for 40 minutes. Leave to cool, then transfer onto a serving plate.

Carciofi alla brace

Barbecued artichokes

In Italy, when I was young, roasted artichokes were sold by the roadside when in season. The aroma and the fumes were so intoxicating that you just had to stop and buy some. I recreated these on my barbecue at home; they were wonderful and brought back many memories. Why not try them on your barbecue for something different this summer?

12 SERVINGS

12 medium-sized artichokes

6 handfuls of parsley, finely chopped

4 garlic cloves, finely chopped

salt and pepper, to taste

10 tablespoons extra-virgin olive oil

12 tablespoons water

Light the barbecue and allow it to burn down a little until it is a gentle heat.

Prepare the artichokes: cut off the stalk, leaving about 4cm attached to the artichoke, and finely chop this removed section.

In a bowl, mix together the parsley, garlic and finely chopped stalk, adding some salt and pepper to taste. Fill each artichoke heart with this mixture. Stand them upright on the barbecue when it is at a gentle heat, and drizzle with the olive oil and with about a third of the water. Cover with aluminium foil and leave to cook for approximately 1 hour.

Check from time to time, adding a little water, if needed. The artichokes are cooked when the outer leaves are burnt. Remove from the barbecue, discard the burnt leaves, sprinkle with some salt and serve.

Tip: You can also roast them in the oven, just follow the same method as above. Heat the oven as high as it will go, up to 250°C/480°F/gas 10 and then, when the artichokes are ready to go in, reduce to 220°C/425°F/gas 7 and roast for about an hour.

Spiedini di carne mista con varieta' di vegetali
Barbecued mixed meat and vegetable skewers

Italians love to eat barbecued *spiedini* during the long warm summer, and they like to vary them with meat, vegetables, fish, and even cheese. In this recipe, I have included three different types of meat, but you can substitute according to your tastes and preferences. You can buy Italian sausage from any good Italian deli. These skewers are perfect for summer barbecues and are delicious with *Rice Salad* (see page 175).

MAKES APPROX. 12 X 30CM SKEWERS

FOR THE MARINADE

100ml white wine

5 tablespoons extra-virgin olive oil

salt and pepper, to taste

2 sprigs of rosemary

1 teaspoon fennel seeds

500ml good-quality fresh Italian pork sausage, cut into 3cm chunks

500ml free-range chicken breast, cut into 3cm chunks

500ml lamb fillet, cut into 3cm chunks

1 yellow pepper, cut into squares

1 red pepper, cut into squares

60 bay leaves

1 sprig of rosemary, for basting skewers (optional)

Mix the marinade ingredients together. Place the sausage, chicken, lamb and peppers in a bowl and pour over the marinade. Mix well and leave in the fridge to marinate for 1 hour.

Remove from the fridge. Take the skewers and start threading the food onto them. Begin with a bay leaf, followed by a chunk of sausage, red pepper, chicken, yellow pepper, lamb, bay leaf, red pepper and then sausage again, and continue in this way until the skewer is complete. Make sure you leave approximately 4cm clear at either end so that it is easy to pick up. Continue to do this until all the skewers are finished and the ingredients are used up.

Make sure your barbecue has burnt down to a gentle heat, place the skewers on its grill and cook, turning them over as each side is done. If you have any marinade left, you can baste the skewers using a sprig of rosemary. Leave on the heat until all the meats are properly cooked through, and serve.

Tip: Make sure your barbecue is NOT too hot when you put the skewers on the grill, otherwise you will burn the meat and peppers (as we did!) and risk not cooking them all the way through.

Prosecco alla pesca

Peach Prosecco

In the summer months as the first peaches ripen, it is traditional in Italy to put them in white or red wine, which is then placed in the fridge for a few hours or so. During mealtimes we drink the peach-infused wine and later enjoy the peach for the dessert course. This practice gave me the idea for this recipe, which is a deliciously refreshing drink at parties, or served as an aperitif prior to lunch or dinner.

8 SERVINGS

8 medium-sized, firm peaches (discard the stone and cut into quarters)

3 litres dry white wine

2 bottles of Prosecco, well chilled

Place the quartered peaches in a large container and top with the white wine. Seal the container and place it in the fridge for about 4 hours.

Drain the peaches, put a couple of chunks in a glass and top with chilled Prosecco. *Salute!*

Tip: Do not throw away the strained wine; you can drink it with meals as I have described above, or pour it into a punch bowl with some of the sliced peaches to serve to guests.

Tip: I like to keep the skin on the peaches in this recipe but if you prefer, you can remove them by blanching for about a minute or so, making it easy to take off the skin.

Aranciata sanguinello
Blood orange juice

You can't get more organic than this orange juice! I like to make this during the winter months when blood oranges are in season; that way I can preserve their sweet, delicate taste longer. If you can't get the blood-red variety, you can use ordinary oranges, or even with other citrus fruit, such as mandarins, lemons or pink grapefruit.

This is a perfect, healthy drink for children and adults, and below I have suggested a few ideas for how you can serve it. Please note that the amount of juice you obtain from the oranges varies, therefore you should follow this formula: for every litre of juice obtained, add 600g of sugar. If you follow the recipe below and use 3 kg of oranges, don't be surprised if you get more or less juice – it all depends on the quality of the oranges and their juiciness.

MAKES APPROX. 1.5 LITRES

3kg blood oranges (to give approx. 2 litres of juice)

1.2kg sugar

rind of 2 blood oranges

Sealable bottles (sterilised by being boiled in water for about 5 minutes)

Wash and dry the oranges. Squeeze the oranges well and then, using a sieve, strain the juice produced.

In a saucepan, place the strained juice together with the squeezed orange halves and the sugar. Stir with a wooden spoon and gently bring to the boil, stirring all the time, and cook for 5 minutes. Remove from the heat, add the rind, cover with a lid and leave to rest for 15 minutes. Remove the squeezed orange halves and strain the juice through a sieve. Press the orange halves in a fine sieve and you should find that quite a bit more juice will come out.

Using a funnel, pour the juice into sterilised bottles, leave to cool, then close their lids. Leave the juice to rest for at least 24 hours, after which time it is ready to consume.

How to use: As this is pure concentrate, you need to dilute it with mineral water (either fizzy or still) before serving. It can also be added to Prosecco or champagne for a refreshing pre-dinner or party drink, or you can serve it as a punch with fizzy water and a selection of chopped fruit – perfect for a children's party! For an alcoholic punch, add white wine and chopped fruit.

Limoncello
Lemon liqueur

I am sure you have all heard of the lemon liqueur, limoncello, which is famous on the Amalfi Coast where the wonderful, flavoursome lemons grow. This is a traditional liqueur that all Italians used to make at home – and still do, despite the numerous producers who make this drink in volume quantities. The Amalfi Coast lemons, known as 'sfusato Amalfitano' really are the best; they are untreated, their zest is pungent and full of flavour and their juice is just right – not being too acidic, like a lot of other lemons. These Amalfi lemons are difficult to find outside Italy, but occasionally you can find them at London's Borough Market; otherwise, buy unwaxed organic lemons.

Served chilled, limoncello makes a lovely after-dinner drink. It is also useful in cooking, especially for game dishes or desserts. Try pouring it over good-quality vanilla ice cream. Delicious!

MAKES 2.5 LITRES
6 small, unwaxed lemons
1 litre plain pure alcohol
1.5 litres water
800g sugar

Wash the lemons in cold water then dry well. With a small, sharp knife, carefully remove the lemon peel, making sure you don't leave any of the white bits. (If you do, cut them out.) Place the peel in a large jar, pour the alcohol over and seal hermetically (see tips for preserving on page 225). Place in a cool, dry place for 7 days.

Place the water in a pan over the heat and bring to the boil, add the sugar and stir to dissolve. Remove and allow to cool.

Open the jar and strain the lemon-infused alcohol through a fine sieve, discarding all the peel. Add the alcohol to the sugared water and mix well. Leave to cool completely, then pour into clean, dry bottles. Seal with lids and store in a cool, dry place for 10 days.

Enjoy served cold!

Tip: Always keep a bottle in the fridge and a few small liqueur glasses at the ready in the freezer.

Pane
Bread

There are few things in the world more satisfying than bread. For thousands of years it has been the principal staple of virtually every country in the world, and will probably remain so for thousands more. The scent of bread fresh from the oven is one of the most tantalising aromas known to man. I don't think it matters who first planted wheat, who first made wheat into flour, who invented the sieve, or who pioneered the use of yeast. The fact remains that bread has always existed and satisfied appetites around the world.

There was a time when people had bread to eat, and little else; it is one of the basic foodstuffs of human life.

Bread is healthy and nutritious; it fills the stomach and feeds the soul. Every country has its own way of making bread, but the basic ingredients are still the same, and are brought together with the same magic and in the same sacred ritual. In Italy every town and small village has its own bakers. In towns the bakery is called the *panettiera*; in a small village, simply *forno* (oven). In Italian households bread is served at virtually every meal. Years ago, when not every family had an oven at home, boys used to carry their family's precious cargo of bread dough to the baker's shop on planks of wood covered with tea towels, and after delivering it would wander off with daydreams of smelling the hot, freshly baked loaves they would be taking home. Their mothers would always add in some little bit of sweet baking for the baker to put in the oven for the boys. All this was part

of daily life, and if, on occasion, the bread didn't turn out well, the baker would certainly get an earful from his disappointed customers.

And still today, it is not hard to find families gathered around the dinner table enjoying meals prepared in the town *forno* – for free, of course, as always. Often the ingredients for a special bread would be sent to the shop the day before – eggs, salami, cheese, pepper, pork fat – and the baker would fold them into the dough to make enriched breads for special occasions. Even my mother, near the end of her life when almost all of us had left the family home and she rarely lit up the big oven, used to make up festive breads for us when she knew that we would all be home for the holidays – with a special stuffing and a special decoration for each child. She would give the baker strict instructions on the oven temperature to use for each loaf, and to make sure there would be no mix-ups, she put an identifying mark on each bread.

Bread was never thrown out, not even if it was stale: that was a sin. Perhaps it was the memory of the war, when food was scarce, or maybe just out of respect, since bread was traditionally considered a gift from God. And heaven help you if you put the bread on the table upside down: that brought bad luck! I still think that way. Whether you believe in these things or not, you can still find people who, when they move, take with them to their new house a piece of old bread for good luck, and a chip of wall plaster.

Because bread means tradition.

And the tradition remains, from days past, that when the village celebrated the feast day of its patron saint, volunteers would go round with big baskets on their shoulders filled with votive breads in various shapes and distribute them to the houses and shops in exchange for an offering. Sometimes the bread is simply marvellous, at other times less so, but that isn't the point, because everyone knows that making bread – giving life to flour and water – is a mysterious thing.

I would be happy if what I am writing here summons up a bit of the magic that I feel in the air when I mix up the ingredients to make breads, focaccias, pizzas, rolls, sweet doughnuts and savoury buns – in short, everything you can make with simple ingredients like flour, water, yeast and salt.

I think I should have been a baker. I find making bread such a pleasure, and it's not difficult at all. The essential ingredient is enthusiasm. I think everyone should have a go at baking a loaf of bread at home. There is nothing like the smell of a fresh loaf when it comes out of the oven. I am lucky to have a garden where I have built an outdoor kitchen and wood-burning oven, just like the one from my grandfather's big house in Minori. It's my favourite place to be, because when I am there, it is like I have travelled back in time. And when I get lost in nostalgia for my childhood, this little corner of the yard fills me with warm feelings. When I light the wood inside the oven I hear the crackling of the fire speaking to me – and I feel better.

Then, after making sure the oven temperature is right, kneading the dough and waiting for it to rise, standing in front of the oven with my family all around me, that's when I feel at the centre of the world. I am sure that in years to come my family will remember these moments, too, and that makes me very happy.

Baking in a wood oven might well be the most romantic way to bake, but it is certainly not the easiest. You need to spend a certain amount of time together, you and the oven, to create the right conditions of 'intimacy' between the two of you. But for those of you without a wood oven outdoors, a gas or electric convection oven indoors will be just fine. And instead of the old traditional Italian *madia* (kneading trough) your dough can be worked on a table, or in a bowl. Try to use good, strong, plain flour and if possible live brewer's yeast, which you can usually find in the bread-making section of your local supermarket. Remember never to put salt in direct contact with the yeast, or the bread won't rise as quickly. The dough that you make can be used not just for bread, but also to make excellent pizzas that can be stuffed or fried, or slices of bruschetta to be flavoured with tomatoes, garlic, cheese, anchovies or green vegetables.

And all of this you can create yourself, magically, with your own hands, by kneading and shaping. And if you think about it, these same simple gestures have changed little since the time of your ancestors.

Impasto per il pane

Basic bread dough

I have to write something about bread dough in this book. I grew up watching my mother and my sisters making it, and while they prepared the table for dough-making I would walk around the house in a reverie, dreaming of the tastes of the small pizzas and focaccias that were to come. When my mother made dough she would always give me a piece to make into whatever shape I wanted – and she knew that I would always secretly add in a bit of old cheese to create the perfect bait for fishing. I saved myself a lot of time that way, not having to hunt quite so many worms – worms that I used to show off to my little sister and make her squirm with disgust. Sometimes I didn't have time to go fishing and I would forget about the dough that I had hidden somewhere. Searching for it used to drive my mother crazy!

MAKES 2 LOAVES

25g fresh yeast

700ml lukewarm water

800g oo flour (or strong plain flour)

200g semolina

20g salt

Dissolve the yeast in the lukewarm water. On a clean work surface or in a large bowl, mix together the flour, semolina and salt and pour in the dissolved yeast liquid. Mix well until you obtain a soft, but not sticky, dough. Lightly flour a clean work surface and knead the dough well for about 5 minutes or until smooth and elastic. Place the dough on a clean tea towel, brush the top with some water to prevent it from drying out, then cover with another clean tea towel. Leave to rise in a warm place for about 30 minutes or until the dough has doubled in size.

When risen, either shape the dough into two loaves or into whatever shape you wish. Leave to rise in a warm place for a further 30 minutes.

Preheat the oven to 250°C/480°F/gas 10. When the loaves have risen, reduce the oven to 240°C/465°F/gas 9 and bake for approximately 20 minutes or until golden. To test if the bread is ready, gently remove the loaf from the tin and tap it on the bottom: if it sounds hollow, it is ready. Remove from the oven and leave to cool – even though it is so tempting to slice as soon as you can handle it and spread it with butter! (My girls love doing this!)

The bread will keep for about a week, or even longer, and at the end of that time it can be sliced and made into bruschetta (see page 162–5) or simply toasted.

Focaccia al tartufo con cipolle e patate
Truffled onion and potato focaccia

The idea of this recipe came to me whilst reminiscing over past culinary experiences. A few years ago, I was making focaccia in the Neal Street Restaurant and erroneously put in truffle oil instead of extra-virgin olive oil. I hadn't noticed, and it was not until staff lunch that people began to comment that the focaccia was sublime. That incident inspired me to make a focaccia with truffle oil, and the combination of this with potatoes and onions is excellent!

If you don't like truffles, you can, of course, substitute olive oil for the truffle oil; but if you really like truffles and want a treat, invest in a small black truffle and shave it just before serving!

10 SERVINGS

½ quantity of basic bread dough (see page 194)

3 tablespoons truffle oil

12 tablespoons extra-virgin olive oil

4 large onions, sliced

salt and pepper, to taste

leaves from 4 thyme sprigs

3 tablespoons white wine

700g potatoes, thinly sliced and parboiled

1 tablespoon coarse sea salt

some black truffle shavings (optional)

1 baking tray approx. 36cm long and 30cm wide, sprinkled with flour or semolina

Make the dough as described on page 194, but add 1 tablespoon of truffle oil when mixing in the yeast. Leave to rise for 30 minutes.

Preheat the oven to 250°C/480°F/gas 10. Heat 10 tablespoons of olive oil in a frying pan, add the onions, salt, pepper and thyme leaves. Lower the heat and cook until they have softened. Towards the end of the cooking time, add the wine. Ensure the onions do not burn, then carefully add the parboiled potato slices, taking care not to break them up, and leave to infuse with the onion for a few minutes. Remove from the heat and set aside.

Once the dough has risen, place it on a lightly floured, clean work surface and roll it out into a roughly rectangular shape the size of the baking tray. Place the dough on the baking tray and then, using your fingers, make indentations all over it. Spread the remaining 2 tablespoons of olive oil all over and brush it round the edges, then sprinkle with the coarse sea salt.

Place the onions and potatoes, including the olive oil they were cooked in, all over the dough. Cover with a cloth and leave in a warm place to rise for 30 minutes.

Reduce the oven temperature to 220°C/425°F/gas 7. Place the focaccia in the hot oven for 30–35 minutes or until evenly golden around the edge.

Remove from the oven, drizzle with the remaining 2 tablespoons of truffle oil and sprinkle with black truffle shavings, if desired. Cut the focaccia into squares and serve immediately. This is delicious eaten warm, but it can be made in advance and then heated through in the oven before serving.

Pane alle erbe e mozzarella

Herb and mozzarella bread

My family would make bread and fill it with whatever was around – bits of cheese, ham, salami or vegetables – and we would traditionally take it on picnics. This is a new version that is made into a loaf and is, I must say, much lighter with the herbs and mozzarella. It is really delicious, and once you have had a slice you just have to have another, and another. If you manage to keep it for longer than a day, it does stay soft and fresh for about 4 days.

MAKES 1 LOAF

15g fresh yeast

300ml lukewarm water

500g strong plain flour

6 tablespoons olive oil

2 teaspoons sugar

1 teaspoon salt

1 large shallot, finely chopped

1 egg, beaten

100g hard mozzarella, finely cubed

6 tablespoons mixed fresh herbs (parsley, thyme, chives and sage)

25g pine kernels, finely chopped

1 tablespoon pine kernels, left whole

salt and pepper, to taste

1 rectangular loaf tin, 22cm x 10cm

Dissolve the yeast in a little of the lukewarm water. In a large bowl, sift the flour, make a well in the middle and pour in the dissolved yeast, 2 tablespoons of the olive oil, the sugar and the salt. Start to mix it, gradually adding more lukewarm water until you obtain a smooth dough. Place the dough on a lightly floured, clean work surface and knead for 10 minutes. Return it to the bowl, cover it with a clean cloth and leave it to rest in a warm place for about 30–40 minutes or until the dough has doubled in size.

Preheat the oven to as close to 250°C/480°F/gas 10 as your oven will go.

Meanwhile, make the filling: heat 2 tablespoons of olive oil in a frying pan, add the shallot and cook until softened. Remove from the heat and allow to cool. Add the beaten egg, the mozzarella, herbs, chopped pine kernels and salt and pepper and mix until it is well amalgamated.

Roll out the dough on a lightly floured, clean work surface into a roughly rectangular shape 1cm thick. Divide the herb filling into two: spread one part on one side of the dough leaving 3cm clear around the edges, then do the same on the other side. The centre should not have any filling. Sprinkle the whole pine kernels over the filling and drizzle with the remaining olive oil. Roll one side until you reach the centre, then roll the other side until the two meet. Place in the loaf tin, cover with a cloth and leave to rise in a warm place for a further 20 minutes.

Reduce the oven temperature to 180°C/350°F/gas 4. Bake in the bottom part of the oven for 50 minutes to 1 hour or until golden brown.

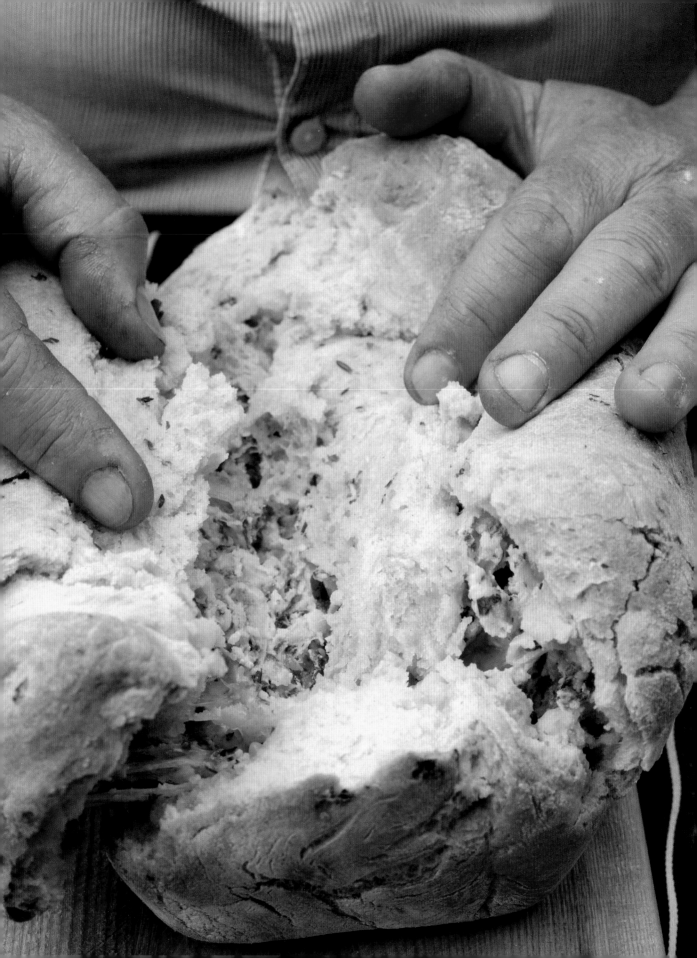

Pizzette alle uova di quaglia e pancetta

Individual pizzas topped with quails' eggs and bacon

Apart from being a perfect snack, this recipe can also be a perfect breakfast. The main ingredients are eggs and bacon, and what is more English than that? I know I always preach about authenticity of pizza, and I am still of that opinion, but this idea came to me one Sunday when my 4-year-old daughter, Olivia, wanted pizza for breakfast. We all laughed, but I had some leftover dough so I came up with this dish, which she absolutely loved. In fact, we all did!

MAKES APPROX. 16 SMALL PIZZAS

FOR THE DOUGH
½ quantity of basic bread dough (see page 194)

FOR THE TOPPING
1 x 400g tin of plum tomatoes (finely chopped and mixed with 2 teaspoons dried oregano)

salt and pepper, to taste

8 tablespoons good-quality Cheddar cheese, freshly grated

8 thin slices of bacon, cut into very fine strips

8 tablespoons extra-virgin olive oil

16 quails' eggs

First, make the dough. Divide it into 16 pieces and leave to rise for a further 30 minutes.

Preheat the oven to as close to 250°C/480°F/gas 10 as your oven will go.

Roll out each piece of dough to a thickness of approximately 5mm and make it into a round pizza shape, approximately 10cm in diameter. Place the pizza bases on non-stick baking trays and spread about 1 tablespoon of tomatoes on each, leaving a small space in the centre (this is for the egg, later on). Season with salt and pepper, sprinkle some Cheddar on each, lay over a few bacon strips and drizzle each pizza with a little olive oil.

Bake in the oven for about 5 minutes, then remove, crack open the quails' eggs over the centre of each pizza. Return to the oven for a couple of minutes until the egg is set. Remove, sprinkle some freshly ground black pepper over the egg and serve.

Friselle
Long-lasting bread rings

Friselle traditionally originate in the Southern Italian region of Puglia, and they were made by the housewife to store for when fresh bread ran out. They are double-baked so that they will harden and therefore last longer – provided they are stored properly. To consume, they have to be softened by being sprinkled with water then drizzled with extra-virgin olive oil, salt and perhaps some herbs and slices of fresh tomato. They are ideal served in hot soups, and if soaked in some water they can be used in the traditional Italian tomato salad known as *Panzanella*.

MAKES APPROX. 12 BREAD RINGS

40g fresh yeast

380ml lukewarm water

800g strong plain flour

a pinch of salt

3 tablespoons fennel seeds (optional)

Dissolve the yeast in a little of the lukewarm water. Mix together the flour, salt and fennel seeds, if using, and place on a clean work surface. Make a well in the centre and add the yeast and water, gradually adding more until you obtain a smooth, soft dough. (If necessary, add more water.) Knead for about 10 minutes. Leave to rise in a warm place for 30 minutes, covered with a cloth.

Place the dough on a lightly floured, clean work surface and roll it into a long sausage shape, cutting out 24 pieces. Roll each piece with your hands until it measures approximately 1.5cm wide and 25cm long. Shape each 'sausage' into a ring, overlapping the ends slightly and pressing them together to seal. Gently flatten each one with your hands, then place another ring on top so that you end up with 12 rings.

Preheat the oven to 240°C/465°F/gas 9.

Leave the dough rings to rest in a warm place for 30 minutes or until they have doubled in size.

Reduce the oven temperature to 180°C/350°F/gas 4. Place the rings on a baking tray and cook in the oven for about 15 minutes. Remove from the oven, slice each *frisella* in half, return to the oven and leave to bake for a further 40 minutes or until they become golden and hard. Turn off the oven and open its door, leaving the *friselle* inside. This way they cool down gradually.

Remove and, once cool, they can be consumed or stored in an airtight container for a couple of weeks. Beware, they are hard, so unless you have vampire-like teeth, I recommend you soften them in a little water before eating!

Pane con i fichi, uva e noci

Bread with figs, grapes and walnuts

During the fig season it was very common to see people eat fresh fruits with hunks of newly baked bread for breakfast. This was especially true of the farm workers, who would bring their own bread and pick fresh figs from the tree – they act as jam on the bread. I still do this today, even in England, when figs are in season. Hence, the idea of this recipe which I have made using dried figs, available all year round, along with the addition of walnuts (another of my favourite foods) and fresh grapes. Lovely to eat freshly baked or toasted the next day with butter.

MAKES 1 ROUND LOAF

½ quantity of basic bread dough (see page 194)

200g dried figs, finely chopped

150g walnuts, finely chopped

200g white grapes, quartered

Follow the basic bread recipe, but reduce the quantity of salt used to half a teaspoon. When you mix the flour, semolina and salt, also add the figs and walnuts and continue to follow the recipe.

Once you have a dough, make it into a ball shape and leave it in a warm place to rise for 30 minutes.

Afterwards, knead the dough again for a couple of minutes, then stretch it and add the grapes, making sure they are evenly distributed throughout. If any grapes are showing, gently poke them back into the dough.

Form into whatever loaf shape you desire, place on a large, flat, baking tray or a loaf tin, cover with a cloth and leave to rise for a further 30 minutes or until it has doubled in size.

Preheat the oven to 230°C/450°F/gas 8.

When the loaves have doubled in size, place them in the hot oven for 35–40 minutes or until cooked. Remove from the oven, leave to cool and serve.

Prodotti Sott'olio e Marmellate

Preserves

Preserving food is an important job in the traditional Italian kitchen; it is a way of keeping the scents and flavours of produce long after they are in season.

When I was growing up in Italy the larder would be full of aubergines and peppers preserved in oil and vinegar, courgettes preserved in oil, tomatoes dried in the hot summer sun, bottles of chopped plum tomatoes and terracotta dishes containing our version of tomato purée (which is a very thick and concentrated paste, which was covered with basil leaves and oil). There would also be various beans in oil, baby artichokes, mushrooms, tuna, anchovies in salt, sun-dried figs, cherries in alcohol, chestnuts, walnuts, jams, home-made liqueurs and oils infused with different herbs. The variety of produce packed into their different containers was a feast for the eyes, as well as the stomach!

Nowadays in Italy, despite the use of freezers, it is still traditional to preserve a lot of produce. Towards the end of summer, work begins when the food is still in season and just right to be prepared for storing. Years ago, this preserved food was the staple filling for sandwiches, and it was common to see farmers going to work in the fields with bread and preserved aubergines or peppers or anchovies. They did not have the variety we have today, but they had the food that they knew was good and wholesome.

In my family, and in many others, preserved produce is not only made for themselves, but also for other members of the family who live further away, and to give as presents. I remember my mother would always send me off with jars and containers of different foods after a visit home, and I would always complain, saying they were too heavy to carry, but she would insist. Throughout the journey I would be cursing those heavy bags; however, once back, just looking at them whilst unpacking made me think of my wonderful mother and those lovely, warm, carefree days at home, and when I eventually got to eat them it was as if I was back in Italy!

Preserving tomatoes was very important years ago because hardly any products were imported and there weren't many companies that did this job. Therefore the tomato, the most essential ingredient in Italian cooking, had to be preserved. The preparation for this annual event took place a couple of weeks before and all the family members were involved. It required quite a bit of organisation, as we had to preserve kilos and kilos of tomatoes to last us the whole winter.

I always remember my mother would have a quiet word with all the female members of the family, and I could not understand why. With time and age, I understood. It was said, in those days, that any female who was menstruating at this time was not allowed to touch the preserves, or else they would go bad! It just goes to show how seriously everyone viewed this preparation process and how important it was to them.

As everything was recycled in those days, the process began with the washing of the jars and bottles. Then, as a team, everyone was given a task: slicing tomatoes, filling the containers, sprinkling over the tomatoes with salt, adding basil leaves or sealing the containers. My job was, nearly always, to push the tomatoes as far down as possible into the bottles, which I would do using long basil stems.

Large tin drums with hot, boiling water were used to pasteurise the tomatoes and these were lit by fire or with gas. As this was done outdoors, the smell of wood burning and tomatoes pasteurising filled the village and I can still remember that familiar smell.

This was always a joyful time in our family, and I always remember my mother's happy, smiling face lovingly keeping an eye on my sisters and I, observing our reaction to this ritual, whilst rapidly moving her hands as she worked.

On balconies and terraces and throughout the village, trays of salted tomatoes sliced in half could be seen as they dried in the hot summer sun. Last year, when I was on holiday in Crete, I decided to do the same and got my partner Liz and my little girls to help: Liz sliced, Olivia salted and Chloe put the tomatoes on trays to dry out on the balcony. Once dried, I put the tomatoes in jars with garlic, basil and olive oil. I brought them back to London, and during the bleak winter months we could still enjoy a little of that Cretan warmth through the delicious tomatoes! They also served as presents; instead of the usual shop-bought souvenirs one brings home to friends, I gave them a jar of my own holiday sun-dried tomatoes! I am so glad that I can still recreate those traditions and pass them on to my children to learn.

The sun-drying of figs was also very important, as no Christmas table would be complete without them. These too were placed on trays on balconies and terraces, soaking up the last of the summer sun. They would be turned over frequently, then brought indoors in the evening so as not to be damaged by the early morning dew. At Christmas time, these dried figs were filled with nuts and lemon and orange peel, drizzled with some white wine and baked. Delicious!

In many families, another tradition was to fill a large container (*tinozza*) with pure wine vinegar and each day you put in whatever produce you could find: small aubergines, baby bell peppers, cauliflower florets, small cucumbers, green baby tomatoes, carrots or pieces of celery. These would be preserved in the vinegar and used as pickled vegetables throughout the winter.

Even fish was preserved: from anchovies in salt to tuna in olive oil. To do this the fish had to be extremely fresh. Years ago, anchovies and tuna were washed in seawater before use, which gave you the real taste of the sea – this was, of course, in the days before pollution. I remember my father waiting on the beach for the boats to come in, eagerly awaiting the fishermen so he could buy the best tuna, anchovies, sardines, or whatever else they had caught. Tuna was quartered and cut on the beach, and what could not be used was thrown back in the sea – now that's what I call recycling! As a boy I was absolutely fascinated by what the fishermen were doing and I was always amazed that they would eat the tuna liver. (Apparently raw tuna liver is good for virility. I have never tested this theory, but it could explain the fact that fishermen's families were always very large!) I still like to preserve tuna today at home in England, where I don't go to the beach to buy the fish, but I can get good-quality tuna from the fishmonger.

I know you can find fresh produce all year round now, but I still love to preserve food in its season and enjoy it later on in the year. I am always experimenting with different foods: some recipes are okay, and some perhaps don't work. This is one tradition from my childhood which I will not give up, and I hope you will try some of the recipes which follow. It's fun, economical and it means you will always have something to eat in your larder that's different and delicious!

Marmellata di pomodorini verdi

Green baby tomato chutney

At the end of last summer, I had a miraculous crop of baby green tomatoes in my garden which no one had planted. Every day there appeared more and more of them, and my girls, Chloe and Olivia, enjoyed picking and playing with them. My sister, Adriana, was staying with us at the time, and as she hates seeing food wasted, she began chopping down the branches and collecting all the tomatoes. Some she preserved in wine vinegar, some in extra-virgin olive oil and the rest she made into this wonderful chutney. It is delicious spread on fresh bread or eaten with cheese and cold meats.

MAKES APPROX. 1 X 600G JAR OR 2 X 300G JARS

1kg green baby tomatoes

600g sugar

juice of 1 lemon

rind of 1 lemon, cut into strips

sterilised glass jars (this can be done by boiling them in water for about 5 minutes)

Wash the tomatoes, place them in a pan of boiling water and cook for 1 minute. Drain, leave to cool a little, then peel. Cut them in half and discard the seeds. Place the tomatoes in a bowl and add the sugar and lemon juice. Mix well, then leave to marinate for about 8 hours.

Place the tomatoes in a saucepan, add the lemon rind and cook on a medium heat for 1½ hours. Remove from the heat and immediately place in the sterilised jar/s. Seal tightly, turn upside down and leave for 10 hours. After this time, store in a cool, dry place away from sunlight for up to 1 year. Once opened, keep in the fridge for about 1 week.

Finocchi al limone

Lemon-preserved fennel

This is a delicate-tasting preserve which is lovely as part of an antipasto or as a side dish to accompany fish, or simply mixed into a green salad. I have given you the option of flavouring with sage, if you like its strong taste, or mint, which is a little fresher.

MAKES 2 X 1 LITRE JARS OR 4 X ½ LITRE JARS

3 tablespoons coarse sea salt

2kg fennel (trim the tops and wipe the bulb with a clean cloth, quarter lengthways or cut in smaller segments, depending on the size of the fennel)

juice of 3 lemons, plus juice of 1 more, squeezed into a separate bowl

5 pinches of salt

leaves of 2 branches of sage or mint

400ml olive oil

hermetically sealed glass jars (see page 225)

Place 3 litres of water and the coarse sea salt in a large saucepan and bring to the boil. At this point, add the fennel and cook for 5 minutes until tender with bite. Do not overcook!

Drain, but reserve the liquid and leave the fennel to dry on clean kitchen towels. Place the fennel in a large bowl together with the juice of 3 lemons and a pinch of salt. Leave to marinate for one hour.

Remove the fennel from the marinade and divide it between the preserving jars, placing a few sage or mint leaves in each.

Measure out approximately 2 litres of the reserved fennel liquid and strain it through a sieve. Add to this water the juice of 1 lemon and 4 pinches of salt. Pour this liquid three-quarters of the way up into each jar and top with the oil. Close the jars tightly and wrap each one in some old cloth.

To pasteurise, place the jars in a large saucepan together with enough water to cover them. Bring the water to the boil and let it boil on a medium heat for 40 minutes. Should the level of the water drop, add more hot water to top it up. Remove from the heat and leave the jars in the pan of water overnight or for at least 12 hours.

Remove the jars from the pan, wipe them dry and store them in a dark, dry place for about 1 month before consuming. The fennel can be kept in this way for up to 6 months, so make sure you write the date on which you preserved them on a label. Once opened, store in the fridge for up to 7 days.

Ciliege amarene

Preserved morello cherries

Italians like to preserve cherries in the summer when they are in season, as they are not in season for very long and are loved by most people. This recipe uses the morello cherry, which is quite bitter, but when preserved with sugar in the sun they give the most delicious flavour and are used when making desserts and cakes. I know the weather in England is not very predictable, but we have been having hotter summers lately, so you could try this recipe out during a warm spell. Don't worry if it suddenly gets cloudy or it rains, it won't ruin the cherries, but in such conditions do keep them indoors in a warm place. If you do preserve some cherries, you can use them in my recipe for *Italian Cherry Pie* (page 236), simply serve them with some vanilla ice cream, or use the juice for granita or in drinks.

MAKES APPROX.1.5KG

1.5kg morello cherries

1.2kg sugar

1 x 1.5kg, hermetically sealed glass jar (see page 225)

Wash the cherries, remove the stalks and carefully remove the stones, keeping any liquid which drips out. (It's best to do all this over a bowl.)

When all the cherries have been pitted, add the sugar and stir gently with a wooden spoon. Place in the jar, seal the lid and place in a warm, sunny location either on your windowsill or outside. If outside, remember to bring it indoors at night. Give the jar a gentle shake and leave it to rest. Continue to do this for about 10 days or until the sugar has completely dissolved and you obtain a syrup-like consistency. The longer you leave it in the sun, the thicker the consistency.

Of course, if there is no sun, you can still make this recipe and store the jar at home in a warm place where it is exposed to the light.

The cherries can be stored for up to a year, even if opened, but replace the lid after use.

Tip: To make a smaller quantity, the formula is: 800g of sugar for 1kg of cherries.

Tonno in conserva

Preserved tuna

I know we are able to get some really good tinned tuna these days, but I wanted to give you a recipe for making your own which is how my mother used to make it in the days before tinned tuna was available. In those days we had to preserve the fish because we could only get fresh tuna during the spring and summer months. Because tuna is so healthy, my mother insisted on preserving lots of it so that we always had some in our store cupboard. Fresh tuna is widely available now at all fishmongers and even supermarkets, but please make sure the tuna is very fresh before preserving it.

MAKES 1.5KG

1.9kg fresh tuna

210g coarse sea salt

3 litres water

abundant extra-virgin olive oil or good-quality seed oil

1 x 1.5kg sterilised jar (see page 225)

Cut the tuna into large chunks and place them in a large saucepan together with the salt and water. Bring to the boil, then reduce the heat and simmer gently for 3 hours.

Remove the tuna chunks and gently wrap each chunk of tuna separately in kitchen towel and leave to dry overnight.

If necessary, remove the scales and skin. Place the fish in the sterilised jar and fill with olive oil, making sure the tuna is covered.

To pasteurise, seal the jar tightly with the lid, wrap with old tea towels and place in a saucepan of water. Bring to the boil, then reduce the heat to moderate and continue to boil for 30 minutes. Remove from the heat and leave the jar in the water until the water becomes cold.

Remove the jar from the pan and tea towels and store in a cool, dry cupboard away from sunlight. The preserved tuna can be kept for up to 6 months, but once opened, if not all consumed in one go, keep in the fridge for up to 7 days.

Tip: To preserve more or less tuna, the formula is: 70g of salt for every litre of water. It doesn't matter how much tuna you have, the water has to cover it well. I made this recipe with the quantities as above, but these quantities can vary according to the size of saucepan you use.

Antipasto misto sott'olio

Preserved mixed vegetables with anchovies and tuna

MAKES APPROX.
1 LITRE JAR

500g yellow peppers

500g red peppers

1kg aubergines

500g white button mushrooms

500ml white wine vinegar

500ml water

12 black peppercorns

3 cloves

½ handful of fresh parsley, finely chopped

a handful of basil leaves, finely chopped

100g green olives, pitted

200g canned tuna (in extra-virgin olive oil)

100g anchovy fillets

½ small red chilli, finely chopped

200ml tomato passata

2 garlic cloves

abundant extra-virgin olive oil or good-quality seed oil

1 x 1-litre hermetically sealed glass jar (see page 225)

This is a meal in a jar! This recipe includes a selection of vegetables, tuna and anchovies which, when arranged on a dish and served with some good country bread, will give you the perfect antipasto or starter. What could be simpler? You could make a few smaller jars to keep in the store cupboard for those unexpected visitors or to enjoy as a snack at any time. You can substitute vegetables or omit any ingredient if you prefer and make your own version of mixed preserves. Once preserved, they look great on your shelf or cupboard and, of course, once opened they really are tasty!

Wash and clean the peppers, discarding the seeds and white bits, and cut them into strips lengthways.

Wash the aubergines and cut into cubes. Wipe the mushrooms and slice.

Pour the vinegar and water into a saucepan, add the peppercorns and cloves and bring to the boil. Add the yellow peppers and boil for 2 minutes. Drain and leave to dry on kitchen towel. Do the same with the red peppers, aubergines and mushrooms. When leaving them to dry, make sure the vegetables are all well spaced out; they must not be bunched up together.

Mix together the parsley, basil, olives, tuna, anchovy fillets and chilli, add the tomato passata and garlic cloves. Mix well together and add the dry vegetables. Place in the hermetically sealed jar, top with oil so that it covers all the ingredients, and pasteurise (see page 225 for how to do this).

Marmellata di pesche

Peach jam

I dedicate this recipe to Zia Antonietta, the queen of all preserves, but especially her famous peach jam! I happened to be in my home village of Minori last summer and my sister, Adriana, had opened her tiny but wonderful greengrocer shop. At the end of each day, all the unsold fruit and vegetables were never thrown out but were given to my other sister, Carmelina, and Zia Antonietta, who preserved everything. In this way nothing was wasted and everyone had lots of delicious preserves and jams that retained all those wonderful summer flavours. I loved the peach jam, which has kept me going through the winter and I am looking forward to getting more this summer!

MAKES APPROX. 500G

2kg peaches

juice of 2 lemons, strained through a very fine sieve or muslin cloth

800g sugar

1 x 500g sterilised jar, or several smaller jars (see page 225)

Place a large saucepan of water on the heat and bring to the boil. Add the whole peaches and leave for a few seconds. Remove, drain and peel away the skin. (This is an easy way of removing the skin, but you can, of course, simply peel it with a knife if you prefer.) Carry out this procedure over a bowl so as not to lose any of the juice.

Cut the peaches into small pieces and remove the stone. Place in a bowl with the sugar and leave to macerate for 24 hours.

Place the peach pieces in a saucepan with the strained lemon juice, bring to the boil, then reduce the heat to low and gently cook for about 15 minutes, stirring from time to time. Remove and pour the liquid through a sieve. Put the sieved remnants of the peaches back in the saucepan, place on a medium heat and continue to cook, skimming off the foamy residue, until you obtain a jam-like consistency.

Remove from the heat, stir well and pour into a sterilised jar/s. Cover with a lid/s and place in the store cupboard. The jam can last at least a year or two, but once opened keep it in the fridge for up to 7 days.

Pomodori secchi sott'olio

Sun-dried tomatoes in oil

I like to preserve my own sun-dried tomatoes – that way I can choose the extra-virgin olive oil I like and whatever flavouring I wish to add. You can find ready-made sun-dried tomatoes (unless of course you want to sun-dry them yourself the next time we have a really hot summer!) and preserve them at home. They are so useful to have in your store cupboard to serve with antipasto or as a filling in sandwiches.

MAKES APPROX. 3 CONTAINERS OF 250G EACH

1.5 litre water

100ml white wine vinegar

1kg sun-dried tomatoes

extra-virgin olive oil or good-quality seed oil, as required

a handful of fresh basil leaves

½ red chilli, finely chopped

3 x 250g sterilised jars (see page 225)

Put the water and vinegar in a large saucepan and bring to the boil. Add the sun-dried tomatoes and boil for a couple of minutes. Remove, drain and place them well spaced out on a clean tea towel and place another tea towel over the top. Leave to dry for a couple of hours.

Take the sterilised jars and drizzle the bottoms with some of the olive oil. Open up each tomato and press them down flat into the jars. Follow with some basil leaves and a little chilli, then another layer of tomatoes, always pressing down well with your hands. Continue with these layers until you have finished the tomatoes, and press down really well to finish. Top with olive oil, ensuring that all the tomatoes are covered, and seal.

The next day, check the jars to make sure the olive oil has been absorbed by the tomatoes and has reached the bottom of the jars. If necessary, add more olive oil. Check from time to time that the tomatoes are well absorbed with olive oil. The tomatoes can last for more than a year, even once they have been opened, just top up with extra-virgin olive oil, if necessary.

Fichi sprucculati

Dried figs baked in white wine and filled with walnuts and citrus fruit

In Italy it was traditional to make these sweet treats for Christmas, using the figs we had dried at the end of the summer. Nowadays you can find the figs ready dried in shops, and most people use these to make this at home. This is the traditional recipe for *fichi sprucculati* that we used, and my sisters in Italy still make it this way. These figs smell and taste of Christmas and are a healthy sweet treat. They last a long time, too, so they can be made in advance and, if wrapped nicely, make lovely Christmas presents!

MAKES APPROX. 40 FIGS

100g walnuts, finely chopped

zest of 1 large orange, finely chopped

zest of 1 mandarin, finely chopped

4 teaspoons fennel seeds

500g dried figs

24 bay leaves

½ glass white wine

4 x 30cm-long wooden skewers

Place the chopped walnuts in a small bowl together with the orange and mandarin zests and 1 teaspoon of the fennel seeds. Mix together well and set aside.

Split open a fig using a small, sharp knife, keeping it together but allowing it to stay flat. Press into the filling mixture, flesh-side down. Do the same with another fig and press the two together. Continue to do this until all the figs and filling have been used.

Preheat the oven to 160°C/320°F/gas 3.

Take 2 wooden skewers and thread on one bay leaf, followed by two pressed-together and filled figs, follow with another bay leaf and continue until you have 10 pairs of filled figs on one skewer. Repeat the process using the other skewers.

Place the filled skewers in an ovenproof dish and pour over the wine. Gently press the skewers into the wine on both sides. Sprinkle half of the remaining fennel seeds over the figs, then turn them over and sprinkle with the rest.

Place in the oven for about 5 minutes or until the wine has evaporated. Remove, allow to cool, and store in containers in a cool, dry place and use when required.

Tips for preserving

A lot of people shy away from preserving food because of all the rules and regulations concerning sterilising and pasteurising, but there is really nothing to it. Here are a few tips to help:

- Always use very fresh, good-quality fruit and vegetables that are in season.

- When preserving in oil, make sure you are using good-quality extra-virgin olive oil. It may seem expensive, but when the oil is good, it makes the preserved food taste good and when it is finished, you can use the leftover olive oil to dress salads.

- Never use aluminium pots and pans and always use wooden spoons when stirring.

- Use smaller jars: this way, when you open one it is likely that all the contents will be consumed in one go or more quickly than if they are in a large jar which could go off before you get round to eating it all.

- To sterilise jars: wash and clean well all the jars you are going to use and rinse them out with a little white wine vinegar at the end. Leave to drain and dry well. If you are using new jars, after washing you must place them in a large pot of boiling water and boil for a couple of minutes. Remove, drain and dry well.

- To pasteurise: once you have placed your food in the jars, seal them well – preferably with hermetically sealed jars. These are glass preserving jars available from hardware and cookery shops, which tend to have a rubber seal and a strong metal catch to keep the jar air- and water-tight. Wrap each jar in old tea towels so that the jars won't break during cooking. Take a large saucepan and line it with a tea towel, place the wrapped jars in it, add enough cold water to cover the jars and above (about 3cm higher). Bring the water to the boil, then reduce the heat to medium and boil according to your recipe. Turn off the heat, but leave the jars in the water until the water is cold. At this point, you can remove the jars, unwrap the cloths, dry the jars and place them in your store cupboard.

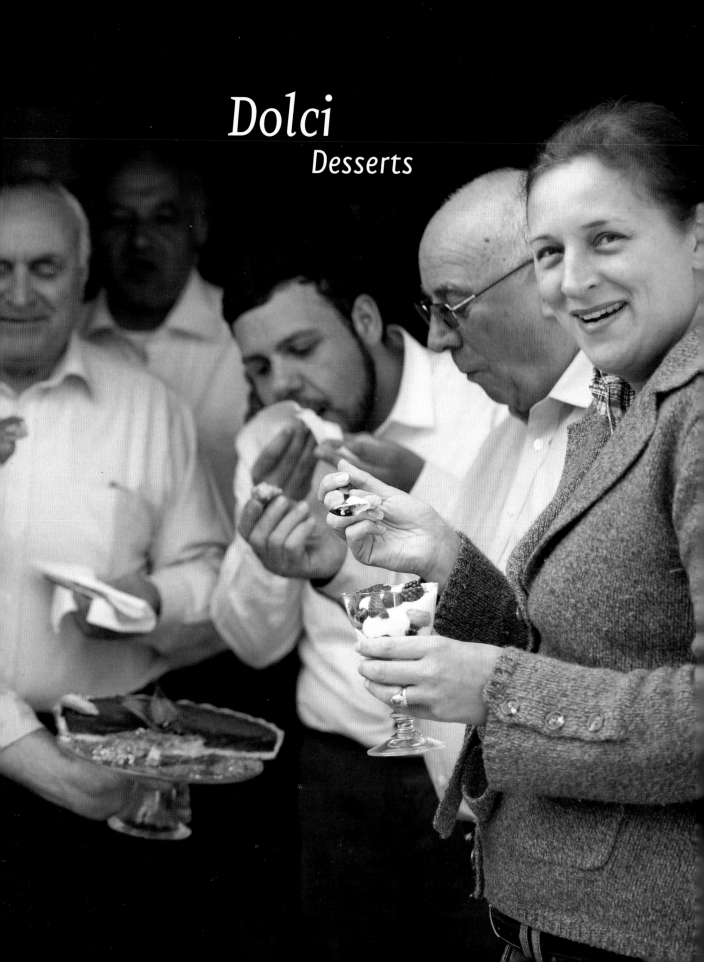

Dolci
Desserts

My earliest childhood memories of desserts always involved fresh fruit. Even today our desserts are based on it and the fruit bowl holds a place of honour in the centre of the table. When I was growing up, sweet, prepared desserts were always made at home and only served on special festive occasions, but with today's large-scale production of sweets and pastries, desserts are now served regularly on Sunday. After the customary Sunday Mass and the ritual promenade by the sea, in all types of weather, it is now almost obligatory to stop at the pastry shop before returning for the big midday meal (*il pranzo*) to buy the classic paper tray laid out with *sfogliatelle*, *cannoli*, *baba' con cream*, *pasticciori* with *amarene*, doughnuts rolled in sugar and cinnamon, cakes and *crostate* (fruit tarts). And so on this day of the week you can see these gift-wrapped trays of pastries being carried down every street in every big or small town in Italy; a sure sign of a good *pranzo* to come.

Both my mother and grandmother had a great passion for making sweets. They used to send me to get the fruit, because I was the one who knew where the best was to be found. I was always the first to climb up onto the fig trees and pick the ripest; I knew when this was because I checked them every day. Cherries, plums, pomegranates, apricots – I knew every tree and the fruit which grew on it. And when it was pomegranate season I even knew which fruit produced the sweetest taste, because the flowers of the pomegranate tree held a special interest for me. These flowers are particularly resilient and I would pick them because I liked their conical shape, and with the help of a straw you could suck up the sweet, almost sugary, taste of the pollen which tingled on your tongue.

Autumn, when chestnuts are in season, is the time to make a cake called *castagnaccio*, using just chestnut flour, olive oil, pine nuts and, for those with a sweet tooth, perhaps

chocolate, too. Autumn is also the time to make pear preserves and jams of persimmon and fig.

Of course, as I explained in the previous chapter, preserves are also made in summer, when fruits such as peaches, apricots and plums and wild berries such as raspberries, blackberries and mulberries are in season. And even before then, in May, my mother used to fill glass jars with morello cherries and sugar and leave them out in the sun for several days until the sugar had dissolved. This sweet, cherry syrup was used to make cherry ices in the summer, or in winter to make *pasticciori*, a traditional sweet pie filled with cream and preserved morello cherries (see page 236). May was also the time for wild strawberries, which I loved to collect for my mother to make into lovely jam.

If the smell of sweet baking in the oven is sublime, that smell was even more enchanting for me because my mother, while cooking, would tell me stories about the sea sirens, about their great beauty and how their singing would cast a spell over seafarers sailing near them. They practised their magic near the island of *Li Galli*, just up the coast from where I lived, and which you could see from the shore on days when the weather turned cooler and the sea mist lifted. Without knowing a line of the *Iliad* or *Odyssey*, my mother would tell me about Ulysses, whose travels brought him right to our coast, attracted by the song of the sirens. And sometimes, when the sea is calm, if you listen carefully to the gentle murmur of the waves, you can still hear that music from ancient times. She also said that when the sea was churned up you could hear a dull sound coming from deep under the sea – the tolling of a large bell that went down with the ship that was transporting it. She passed on to me the magic that still lingers on the Amalfi Coast; its crystal blue waters, breathtaking panoramas, picturesque historic port towns (such as

Positano and Amalfi), and its enchanted isles of Capri and Ischia, are reason enough to justify its status as a World Heritage Site under the protection of the United Nations. I loved hearing her tell me these stories as we worked together in the kitchen and, late at night, when I was in my bed in our big old house by the sea, I would listen hard to see if I could hear the song of the sirens and the tolling of the sunken bell at the bottom of the sea. It was then that I would get a craving for something sweet and would quietly sneak into the larder to seek out any leftover cake or pudding with a mind to create a little bit of music of my own – but this time for my belly!

Tiramisu ai frutti di bosco

Fruits of the forest tiramisu

This is a variation of the traditional Italian tiramisu dessert that has become so popular across the world. Literally translated, *tiramisu* means 'pick-me-up', because this dessert is normally made with strong espresso coffee, which when coupled with the rich mascarpone cream really does make you get up and go! As my little girls don't like the taste of coffee but love berries, I came up with this recipe – and believe me it is very popular in our household. You can, of course, exchange the fruits included here for whatever combination of soft fruit you prefer.

8 SERVINGS

1 punnet each of strawberries, blueberries, raspberries, blackberries (weighing approx. 700g in total)

5 tablespoons sugar

juice of 4 oranges

3 eggs, separated

350g mascarpone cheese

150g Savoiardi biscuits (or use sponge fingers)

8 individual glass bowls or 1 large glass bowl

Wash and pat dry all the berries, then hull and slice the strawberries, leaving the other berries whole. Place all the fruit in a bowl with 2 tablespoons of the sugar and the orange juice. Place in the fridge and leave to macerate for 30 minutes.

Place the egg yolks in a bowl and whisk them with the remaining 3 tablespoons of sugar until light and fluffy (you can do this using either a hand whisk or an electric one). Loosen the mascarpone and add this to the egg yolk mixture, then continue to whisk until well amalgamated and creamy.

Whisk the egg whites in another clean bowl until they form stiff peaks. Using a spatula, carefully fold them into the mascarpone mixture and set aside.

Drain the soaking fruit, reserving their liquid. Quickly dip each biscuit into the liquid for a few brief seconds (making sure they don't become mushy or break), then arrange a layer of them on the bottom of each glass bowl and top with a little of the mascarpone cream, followed by pieces of fruit. Repeat these layers until all the ingredients have been used up, making sure you finish off with some fruit. Keep the tiramisu in the fridge for about 30 minutes or until needed.

Tip: If making for adults, you can add some Cointreau: use the juice of 2 oranges plus 3 tablespoons of Cointreau instead.

Torta di nocciole

Hazelnut cake

8–10 SERVINGS

120g butter, softened at room temperature, plus more for greasing the tin

40g plain flour, sieved, plus more for dusting the tin

6 eggs

150g sugar

170g ricotta cheese

grated zest of 1 lemon

grated zest of 1 orange

150g hazelnuts, roasted, shelled and coarsely ground

1 tablespoon lemon juice

FOR THE GLAZE

8 tablespoons apricot jam

FOR THE TOPPING

50g dark chocolate, thickly grated

6 whole hazelnuts (mixed with a little apricot jam so that they stick together to form a small pile)

a little icing sugar, sieved

TO SERVE

200g mascarpone cheese

2 tablespoons Frangelico liqueur (optional)

3 tablespoons runny honey

1 round, shallow cake tin, 20cm in diameter

This is a mouthwateringly moist cake that is made with ricotta and ground hazelnuts. It is a delight to bake – especially for special occasions when you can get really carried away with the decoration! Although rather rich, it always amazes me how quickly the slices are eaten up each time I make it. It is delicious served as a dessert with the mascarpone cream or a mixed berry coulis, or simply enjoyed with a nice cup of tea!

Preheat the oven to 180°C/350°F/gas 4. Grease the cake tin with a little butter and lightly dust it with flour. Place the tin in the fridge until ready to use.

Separate the eggs and place the whites and yolks in two large bowls. Add 125g of the sugar to the egg yolks and beat well, then add the butter and continue to beat until light and fluffy.

In a separate bowl, beat the ricotta lightly to loosen it. Add this to the egg yolk mixture and continue to beat until well amalgamated. Add the lemon and orange zest. Add the ground hazelnuts and mix well. Fold in the sieved flour.

Take the bowl of egg whites and whisk them together with the remaining 25g of sugar and the lemon juice, until light and fluffy. Fold this carefully into the cake mixture.

Remove the cake tin from the fridge and pour the mixture into it. Bake in the oven for 30–35 minutes. Allow to cool, then remove from the tin and place on a plate.

Stir the apricot jam to loosen it a little and spread it evenly over the top of the cake. Sprinkle with grated chocolate and place a small pile of whole hazelnuts centrally on the top. To finish, lightly dust with sieved icing sugar.

Mix together the mascarpone, Frangelico (if using) and honey to a creamy consistency. Cut the cake into slices and serve with the mascarpone cream.

Biscotti con la marmellata

Jam biscuits

These are my favourite biscuits. Years ago, these biscuits were made at home, and usually we children would take leftover pieces of pastry after my mother had made a *crostata* (tart) and we would cut out different shapes which would go into the oven with Mamma's tart. Nowadays, these jam bicuits are made in *pasticcierie* (pastry shops) and when I am in Italy, a trip to the *pasticcieria* is a must. On my last day there, I always make sure I buy a large boxful of these biscuits to enjoy at home!

I have not specified which jam to use as the filling, as I am sure you have your preference. My favourite is apricot. You could also use a chocolate filling (see the chocolate topping on page 240). You can get the children involved in making these biscuits; my two love rolling out dough and cutting shapes, and they can also choose their own filling!

MAKES 12 LARGE BISCUITS

300g plain flour

200g butter

140g icing sugar

13g sachet of vanilla powder

zest of 1 orange

1 egg yolk

knob of butter, for greasing the baking tray

greaseproof paper, for lining the baking tray

jam of your choice (approx. 2 tablespoons per biscuit)

caster sugar, for sprinkling

1 large, flat baking tray

2 round pastry cutters, 1 x 8cm in diameter, 1 x 5cm in diameter

Sift the flour onto a clean work surface and rub in the butter until it resembles breadcrumbs. Mix in the sugar, vanilla and orange zest. Add the egg yolk and work into a smooth pastry but work quickly to avoid the pastry getting warm. Form the dough into a ball, wrap it in cling film and place it in the fridge for about 2 hours or until required.

Preheat the oven to 160°C/320°F/gas 3 and line a flat baking tray with greaseproof paper.

Remove the pastry from the fridge and unwrap the cling film. Lightly sprinkle some flour onto a clean work surface and roll out the pastry using a rolling pin that is 6mm thick.

Using the larger pastry cutter, cut out 24 circles. Leave 12 where they are and take the smaller pastry cutter and cut out 12 circles from these so that they have holes in the centre. At this stage you could also get the children involved and let them cut out star or flower shapes, as long as they are roughly 5–6cm in diameter.

Place a little jam in the centre of the whole rounds, then place the 'holed' circles on top, sandwiching them together. The jam should be seen, but be careful not to use too much, otherwise it will escape during cooking. Sprinkle a little caster sugar over the pastry.

Place in the oven for about 15 minutes or until lightly golden. Remove, leave to cool, then set on a plate and enjoy!

Pasticciotto d'amarene

Italian cherry pie

And I bet you thought only the English made pies! The *pasticciotto* is a very old Italian dessert which was traditionally baked at home, but now the *pasticcierie* make them. The filling consists of a *crema pasticciera*, which is a type of home-made custard combined with preserved '*Amarene*' cherries (known in Britain as morello cherries and available in good Italian delis). If you can't get hold of *Amarene* cherries, you could try preserving them yourself (see page 214). This Italian cherry pie makes a delicious dessert that doesn't need any cream served with it, as you have everything in the pie!

12 SERVINGS

FOR THE PASTRY

350g plain flour, plus extra for dusting the tin

150g unsalted butter, plus extra for greasing the tin

150g sugar

zest of 1 lemon

4 egg yolks

FOR THE CREMA PASTICCIERA

750ml milk

1 vanilla pod (or 13g sachet of vanilla powder)

9 egg yolks

300g sugar

75g cornflour

200g preserved *Amarene* cherries

icing sugar, for dredging

1 egg yolk, beaten, for brushing the pastry (optional)

1 round flan or cake tin, 22cm in diameter and 4.5cm deep

To make the pastry: place the flour in a large bowl or on a clean work surface and rub in the butter until it resembles breadcrumbs. Add the sugar, lemon zest and egg yolks, mixing well until you obtain a smooth pastry. Form into a ball, wrap in cling film and place in the fridge for a couple of hours.

In the meantime, make the crema pasticciera: pour the milk into a small saucepan together with the vanilla pod or the vanilla powder and place on the heat until the milk reaches boiling point. Meanwhile, whisk the egg yolks and the sugar in a bowl until light and fluffy. Add the cornflour and continue to whisk.

When the milk reaches boiling point, remove the pan from the heat and gradually pour the milk into the egg mixture, whisking all the time to prevent lumps forming. Once well amalgamated, pour the mixture back into the saucepan on a medium heat and stir with a wooden spoon. As soon as it begins to boil, remove from the heat (do this very quickly otherwise the cream on the bottom of the pan will burn), and allow to cool. To help it cool more quickly, pour it into a large flat container and stir from time to time.

Preheat the oven to 170°C/325°F/gas 3.

Grease the baking tin with a little butter and dust with flour. Remove the pastry from the fridge. Sprinkle some flour over a clean work surface, roll out the pastry to a thickness of 4mm and line the prepared tin with it. Pour over the cooled cream and top with the preserved cherries, drizzling over a little of the cherry juice. Roll out the remaining pastry and cover the cherries, sealing well around the edges as you would a pie. Brush the pastry top with beaten egg yolk, if using.

Cook in the preheated oven for approximately 50 minutes or until evenly golden.

Remove from the oven and leave to cool. Once cool, remove the pie from the tin, place it on a large serving plate, dredge with some icing sugar, slice and serve.

Castagnaccio con noci, uvetta, pere e cioccolato

Chestnut cake with hazelnuts, raisins, pears and chocolate

I love chestnuts so much, and whilst writing this book I was in Tuscany in the autumn and was able to sample many different versions of this cake, so I could not resist including this recipe. It is a rich cake, but I adore the flavour of chestnuts and here I have combined it with my favourite fruit – pears – some chocolate, raisins and hazelnuts. Try to find the Italian Abate pears, which are perfect for this cake and are available in supermarkets in the autumn. You can substitute Conference pears if you can't get Abate ones, and if you prefer you can use different dried fruits and nuts, omitting those that you don't like. This makes a perfect dessert and is also lovely with afternoon tea.

12 SERVINGS

a knob of butter, for greasing the baking tin

breadcrumbs or flour, to dust the baking tin

400g chestnut flour

80g caster sugar

a pinch of salt

900ml water

4 tablespoons extra-virgin olive oil

2 Abate pears, peeled and cubed

80g dark chocolate, in shavings

40g pine kernels

25g raisins (soaked in a little Grand Marnier then drained)

TO SERVE

icing sugar, for dredging

1 rectangular baking tin, approx. 30cm x 23cm

Preheat the oven to 200°C/400°F/gas 6. Grease the baking tin with the butter and dust lightly with either breadcrumbs or flour.

Put the chestnut flour, sugar and salt in a large mixing bowl and mix together well. Gradually add the water and olive oil, whisking well to prevent lumps forming. Pour the mixture into the prepared baking tin.

Arrange the cubed pears, chocolate shavings, pine kernels and drained raisins over the top of the chestnut mixture, gently pressing each piece with your finger and making sure the pieces don't sink to the bottom.

Cook in the oven for 45 minutes or until a slight crust begins to form on the top of the cake. Remove from the oven and dredge sieved icing sugar over the top. Delicious eaten warm or cold.

Torta di mela di Nonna Genoveffa
Granny Genoveffa's apple cake

In the autumn, when apples were in abundance, I would bring home basketfuls and I always made sure that I gave lots to my grandma, because I knew she would make her delicious apple cake. She would make several batches to give to family and friends; I would always hide a few slices so I could have them for my mid-morning break at school or wherever I was that day!

This is a typical, rustic Italian cake without much butter; not too sweet and full of homey goodness! I have used Granny Smith apples, but any sort will suffice, and if you prefer you can replace them with pears, plums or apricots. There's a cake for every season!

12 SERVINGS

160g unsalted butter, softened, plus extra for greasing tin

greaseproof paper, for lining tin

6 eggs

300g caster sugar

600g self-raising flour

13g sachet of vanilla powder

6 Granny Smith apples, peeled, cored and chopped into medium-sized pieces (to avoid discolouration, leave them in a bowl with a little lemon juice until needed)

zest of 1 small lemon

1 round cake tin, 26cm in diameter, with a loose bottom, if you have one

Preheat the oven to 180°C/350°F/gas 4.

First grease the cake tin with a little butter, then line it with greaseproof paper.

In a large bowl, whisk together the eggs and sugar until light and fluffy. Add the softened butter and continue to whisk until well amalgamated. Sift in the flour and vanilla powder and fold in. Fold in the apples and lemon zest.

Pour the mixture into the prepared baking tin and bake in the oven for 50–60 minutes or until golden. Remove from the oven and allow to cool. Loosen the cake from the tin and place on a serving plate.

Slice and serve with cream, mascarpone or custard for a lovely dessert, or simply enjoy on its own with a cup of tea!

Crostata al cioccolato con pere speziate al vino rosso

Chocolate tart with spiced pears and red wine

This is every chocoholic's dream: a deliciously rich chocolate tart filled with smooth cream and pears cooked in red wine and spices. It is topped with even more chocolate, giving it a perfect shiny finish. This tart takes a little time to prepare, but it really is a simple recipe and can be made in advance. Well worth the effort, this sophisticated dessert is the perfect ending to any dinner party. For best results, I do urge you to buy good-quality dark chocolate.

12 PLUS SERVINGS

FOR THE PASTRY

200g plain flour

75g butter

75g caster sugar

2 egg yolks

FOR THE PEARS

400g Conference pears, peeled and cubed

100g caster sugar

300ml red wine

½ vanilla pod

4 strips of orange peel

4 cloves

2 star anise

1 cinnamon stick

FOR THE FILLING

300ml milk

75ml cream

10g good-quality dark chocolate

3 eggs

60g caster sugar

10g cocoa powder

FOR THE TOPPING

250ml cream

50g glucose syrup

320g good-quality dark chocolate, finely chopped

First make the pastry: place the flour and butter in a large bowl or on a clean work surface. Rub the butter into the flour until it resembles breadcrumbs. Stir in the sugar, then add the egg yolks and mix well until you obtain a smooth, soft dough. Form it into a ball, wrap it in cling film and place it in the fridge for 2 hours or until required.

Preheat the oven to 180°C/350°F/gas 4.

On a clean work surface, roll out the pastry to a thickness of 5mm and line the tin with it. Bake the pastry blind in the oven for 10 minutes or until nearly cooked. Remove and allow to cool. Leave the oven on while you prepare the filling, lowering it to 160°C/320°F/gas 3.

Place the cubed pears in a saucepan together with the sugar, wine, vanilla pod, orange peel and the spices. Bring to the boil, reduce the heat and simmer gently until the pears are tender. Remove from the heat and drain the pears, making sure all the spices, vanilla and orange peel are discarded and the liquid is strained into a bowl. Set aside.

To make the filling: pour the milk and cream into a pan and bring to the boil. Remove from the heat and drop in the chocolate pieces, stirring until they have melted. In a bowl, mix together the eggs, sugar and cocoa powder, then add to the milk and cream. Stir in the wine and spice liquid from the pears and allow to cool.

Take the flan tin with the cooked pastry and arrange the pears over the bottom. Pour over the filling mixture to three-quarters of the way up the sides and place in the oven for about 45–50 minutes or until set. Remove and allow to cool.

Meanwhile, make the topping. In a pan, bring to the boil the

TO DECORATE (OPTIONAL)

a couple of large dried pear slices

grated zest of ½ orange

a handful of chocolate shavings

1 round flan tin, 28cm in diameter and with a loose bottom or, better still, one that opens at the side

cream and glucose, remove from the heat and stir in the chocolate as quickly as you can.

Carefully remove the cooked tart from its tin, place it on a large serving dish and spread over the chocolate topping. Allow the topping to cool, then decorate with dried pears, grated orange zest and chocolate shavings, if you wish.

Tip: Remove the pan from the heat when you stir in the chocolate, otherwise it will go wrong!

Macedonia calda con crema

Warm and creamy mixed fruit

This alternative way to serve chopped fruit makes a lovely dessert. Ensure that you buy good-quality, free-range eggs and cream when making this dish. It is very easy to prepare, and it can be prepared in advance either in small individual dishes or one large dish and placed under a hot grill just before serving. Here I have suggested some fruit to include in this, but you can use whatever sort you like.

8 SERVINGS

2 apples, peeled, cored and cubed

2 pears, peeled, cored and cubed

30 grapes, halved

1 large banana, sliced

2 kiwi, sliced

juice of 2 oranges

1 teaspoon lemon juice

1 tablespoon sugar

100g icing sugar

6.5g vanilla powder

8 egg yolks

100ml whipping cream

extra icing sugar, for dredging

8 shallow ovenproof dishes or 1 large serving dish

Place the chopped fruit in a bowl together with the orange and lemon juice and sugar and leave to macerate while you make the creamy topping.

Place the icing sugar, vanilla powder and egg yolks in a bowl and mix with an electric whisk until light and fluffy.

In another bowl, whisk the cream until you obtain a smooth, creamy consistency (not hard!). Add to the egg mixture and fold in gently.

Drain the fruit well and spoon into one large serving dish or divide between 8 individual bowls. Top with the creamy sauce and place under a hot grill for 2–3 minutes or until golden. Remove, dredge with icing sugar and serve immediately.

Cachi al vino bianco

Persimmons in white wine

Persimmons are a very common fruit in most regions of Italy, and I am pleased to say that they grow in the Campania region where I grew up. They appear from October until Christmas time and are normally picked unripe and kept at home until they are ready to eat. This reddy-orange fleshed fruit is nutritionally very good for you, and I remember as children that we would be given half a persimmon to eat with a little spoon, just as you would an egg! There is also a different variety known to us as *legno santo* (holy wood), which is thus named because we would bite the seeds and often find a shape of a praying hand inside. It was not only delicious to eat, but we had lots of fun to see who had found the most! In England, this fruit is called Sharon fruit, which you can also use for this recipe.

This dish is a very simple way of using persimmons or Sharon fruit and, if you prefer, you can remove the fruit pulp and mix it together with some chopped banana and the wine syrup, then replace it in the cavity so you can enjoy even more fruit and know that you are eating a healthy and tasty dessert!

8 SERVINGS

8 persimmons, ripe, but firm (make sure there are no dark patches on the skin)

80g sugar

juice of 2 lemons

100ml white wine

fresh mint leaves, to decorate

Place the sugar and lemon juice together in a small pan and boil for 2 minutes. Remove from the heat and stir in the wine.

Slice the persimmons in two and score the pulp. Arrange the fruit on a serving dish, pour over the syrup and place in the fridge for a couple of hours or until they are needed.

Remove, decorate with mint leaves and serve.

Menu
Menus

I have now got to the end of this book and, looking back, there are quite a lot of recipes and still many more keep popping into my head. But for now I have to stop! As the theme of the book is about entertaining family and friends, I thought it would be helpful to make up a few menu ideas for main occasions throughout the year, for example, Christmas lunch, parties at different times of the year, picnics and so on. Of course, these are not written in stone and by all means do chop and change and do your own thing, but I hope they help with your menu planning. I wish you Happy Cooking and most importantly, *buon appetito a tutti!*

Christmas lunch

Scallop and wild mushroom salad

Eggy soup

Turkey roasted with pomegranate and orange

Savoy cabbage with chestnuts

Hazelnut cake

Easter lunch

Salad of rocket, broad beans and mozzarella

Semolina gnocchi

Foil-wrapped leg of lamb baked with lemon

Spring vegetables baked in foil

Chocolate tart with spiced pears and red wine

Summer party

Peach Prosecco

Blood orange juice

Rice salad

Grilled polenta bites with salt cod and rocket

Bruschetta with cherry tomatoes and mozzarella

Courgette and mint fritters

Italian cherry pie

Winter party

Prosecco with blood orange juice

Big and hearty antipasto

Parmesan-crusted vegetables

Bruschetta with Parma ham and caramelised figs

Baked pasta

Roast pork with mustard, apple and speck

Dark chocolate fondue

Sweet breadsticks

Children's party

Blood orange juice

Tuna and ricotta crostini

Pork slices coated in walnuts and breadcrumbs

Herby chips

Jam biscuits

Picnic

Herb and mozzarella bread

Pasta omelette

Savoury escarole and smoked mozzarella pie

Watermelon in red wine and citrus fruits

Granny Genoveffa's apple cake

Bonfire-night party

Barbecued mixed meat and vegetable skewers

Braised artichokes with crostini

Truffled onion and potato focaccia

White chocolate fondue with limoncello

Formal dinner (autumn/winter)

Hot garlic and anchovy dip served with raw vegetables

Radicchio and taleggio risotto

Fillets of sole wrapped in Parma ham in a bay leaf sauce

Warm and creamy mixed fruit

Formal dinner (spring/summer)

Aubergine 'parmigiana' with fresh tomato

Broad bean and fennel soup

Seabass with orange

Fruits of the forest tiramisu

Informal get-together (autumn/winter)

Bruschetta with Gorgonzola cheese, walnuts and honey

Soup of spelt with gammon

Beef braised in red wine

Persimmons in white wine

Informal get-together (spring/summer)

Basic bread, cut into slices, either fresh or made into bruschetta

Preserved mixed vegetables with anchovies and tuna

Linguine with aubergine pesto

Sirloin steaks in a tomato and caper sauce

Watermelon in red wine and citrus fruits

Indice

Index